STUDY GUIDE

to accompany

Nash/Jeffrey/Howe/Frederick/Davis/Winkler/Mires/Pestana

THE AMERICAN PEOPLE

Creating a Nation and a Society

Volume One to 1877

Seventh Edition

Prepared by

Thomas F. Jorsch
Ferris State University

PEARSON
Longman

New York Boston San Francisco
London Toronto Sydney Tokyo Singapore Madrid
Mexico City Munich Paris Cape Town Hong Kong Montreal

Study Guide to accompany Nash/Jeffrey/Howe/Frederick/Davis/Winkler/Mires/Pestana, *The American People: Creating a Nation and a Society, Volume One from 1877, Seventh Edition*

Copyright ©2006 Pearson Education, Inc.

ISBN: 0-321-39321-X

1 2 3 4 5 6 7 8 9 10–CW–08 07 06 05

Table of Contents

"A people without history is like wind upon the buffalo grass."
—Lakota

Acknowledgments

The credit for this study guide goes to two groups of people. First, the historians, educators, reviewers, proofreaders, and editors who contributed to the earlier editions of this study guide. Their work, more than my own, shaped the intellectual and physical look of it. Second, the students in history classes who inspired this study guide's creation as a resource to help them understand and find relevance in historical study.

Special thanks are also due to Kristi Olson and Teresa Ward at Pearson Longman. Their editorial and computer skills made the revision of the seventh edition a success.

Thomas F. Jorsch

"The value of History is, indeed, not scientific but moral: by liberalizing the mind, by deepening the sympathies, by fortifying the will, it enables us to control, not society, but ourselves . . . and to meet the future."

—Carl L. Becker

INTRODUCTION

How to Do Well in Your History Course by Rediscovering the Past

In one of Garry Trudeau's "Doonesbury" cartoons, Mike and Zonker are strolling through the woods as Zonker reminisces about their college days. Among other things, he says, they went on study dates in the boat house, held midnight sledding parties, parked the dean's Volvo inside the chapel, got busted at a rock concert, and ran naked through a meeting of the board of trustees. After listening to Zonker's recollections of those "bright college years," Mike reminds him that "we never did any of those things." Zonker agrees, saying, "I know, but one day we'll think we did." "Isn't it a little early to start embellishing?" Mike asks. Zonker coolly responds, "You gotta grab the past while you can!" We introduce the Study Guide to *The American People: Creating a Nation and a Society* with this cartoon for two reasons. First, we are aware that the conflicting demands and pressures of college life often lead students to pranks, pizza parlors, parties, and paper deadline panics—the kinds of events that stimulated Zonker's imagination. Exaggerated and embellished as his fantasies were, they suggest the range of experiences we know students go through, or think about, during their college years. We certainly did. Our current fantasy is that you might add the study of American history to the positive college experiences that you will remember in later years—not made up, like Zonker's, but for real!

We have prepared this Study Guide, therefore, to smooth your way through the American history textbook, not as a substitute for it but as a supplement—a guide to reading *The American People* for maximum understanding, appreciation, enjoyment, and, yes, success on examinations. To be sure, you have many long hours of reading, reflection, and study ahead of you. Studying history is not easy. But it can be pleasurable as well as profitable, and we sincerely hope that you will find your study of American history almost as enjoyable—and certainly as educational—as the diversions that Zonker imagined as a college student.

We also introduce this Guide with Trudeau's cartoon because the last lines say something significant not only about students but also about historians. Although professionally committed to telling the truth about the past, which for the most part they succeed in doing, historians tend sometimes, like Zonker, to "embellish." Like any good storytellers, historians enjoy building an exciting drama by the addition of juicy adjectives and heightened tension. Occasionally they even get a date or name wrong. At one level this is inexcusable, and historians try to check and doublecheck their facts so as never to make errors. But they are only human, and both the authors of your textbook and your history professor may sometimes embellish or make mistakes. So will you, but your errors will be marked wrong. The ultimate responsibility for "getting the history right," therefore, is yours.

Historians also embellish when they interpret the past, not by telling inflated stories or committing factual errors but simply by showing their human point of view, which is the result of their particular time, place, circumstances, and personal backgrounds. Such factors influence the selection and interpretation of past events. Interpretation is unavoidable, and students should beware of a book or person that claims to be "the truth" rather than one interpretation of the truth.

All works of history, even textbooks, present a point of view reflecting the values, assumptions, and interests of the author. Interpretation differs from a biased presentation in that the latter willfully distorts truth while the former deepens understanding by the process of explaining how and why things happened in the past. This makes the writing (and teaching) of history more than a listing of names, dates, and other facts. The act of interpretation is a humble one, and you should be looking for the interpretive point of view of the authors of your textbook as you read. The Preface is a good place to start.

The history presented in *The American People* is enriched by an interpretive framework. It tells the story of the many ways in which the diverse people coming to this country—whether on foot across the Bering Straits, on rafts across the Rio Grande, or on the *Mayflower,* slave ships, or immigrant steamers—created a cultural mosaic of many societies, and one nation. These individual stories are the history, or "story," of "the American people." Our major goal is to help you both learn and enjoy this story. In the 1990s, as we continue to seek to know who we are by knowing where we came from, we realize that, like Zonker, "you gotta grab the past while you can."

IMPORTANT ASSUMPTIONS TO BE AWARE OF

Toward that end, we have prepared this Study Guide. Your teacher has a similar one. We believe that you should know some of our most important assumptions as we prepared the textbook and these Guides. They are as follows:

1. The authors have tried to write a textbook that is not just a series of historical names, dates, places, and other facts—"one damned thing after another," as someone once described history. Rather, we show history as the story of the daily lives of both ordinary and famous Americans in the past. We have sought to take you inside these lives, to experience the fears, frustrations, and aspirations of the American people.

2. We want you not only to reexperience these lives but also to be confident that you remember what you have studied. When learning history is connected to your own experiences, as well as fun, you tend to do better on tests.

3. We believe that the textbook and Guides are only as good as they are teachable and learnable. We have designed both the text and these guides to be immediately usable, if an instructor desires, for a variety of classroom learning activities and assignments that enrich student learning and the appreciation of American history.

4. We believe that students become historians themselves the minute they open their textbooks and begin to read them. When you consulted your list of classes and other sources in order to discover what history course you signed up for and at what time and in what room it met, you were already acting as a historian, recovering a small piece of your own past in order to understand the present. We have designed a special feature in every chapter, called "Recpovering the Past," to show the variety of ways in which all historians, including yourselves, work to construct the past.

5. We believe that students—all people, in fact—learn best when they begin with a personally compelling human experience, their own or someone else's. This human story suggests further stories, or facts, and some overarching themes and concepts. These are in turn analyzed, interpreted, compared to other facts, applied to other settings, and evaluated. Finally, there must be an opportunity to express what one has learned and to receive feedback on how well. We have structured the textbook and this Guide according to this basic pattern of human learning.

HOW TO UNDERSTAND A CHAPTER

Take Chapter 1, for example, which begins with the story of four powerful women in four different cultures. Through determination, guile, and wisdom, these women shape the culture they are part of and influence the future interaction of these cultures. Their stories give us insight into the cultures that will collide in the Americas. For example, Queen Isabella's religious zeal results in Roman Catholicism becoming dominant in Spain at the expense of Jews and Muslims. This pattern of religious conformity will happen again when the Spanish travel to the New World and the meet Aztec people like Tecuichpotzin.

The brief anecdote about the four women introduces most of the overarching themes and major concepts of Chapter 1: the different cultural values that were evolving in different parts of the world and the active resistance put forward by Native Americans and Africans to European influence. The result of this contact (as told in subsequent chapters) was terrible for the Native Americans, whether living in Spanish-controlled Central and South America or near English settlements in North America, and Africans who mostly came to America as slaves. The anecdote indicates the religious and commercial rivalry between Spain and England in Europe that will lead to colonization and different types of settlements. It also reveals tension felt by Native Americans and Africans to the encroachment of Europeans into their culture and that change would not be accepted passively. In each chapter of the textbook, an anecdote of an ordinary person's life will, like the one about the four women, suggest the major themes of the chapter. These themes are stated in the most important section of each chapter: the paragraphs that follow the opening story and precede the first main topic. Read these paragraphs very very carefully.

The bedrock of history, as many history students have found out to their despair, is composed of facts. Broad historical themes are the handles, or pegs, upon which to hang the many particular facts that make up the past. These facts must be mastered—often by memorization—in order to provide life and substance to the larger themes. In Chapter 1, for example, there are a number of names, dates, places, and terms. Once you are familiar with major concepts like the background of the three cultures bound to collide in the Americas and the active role of Native Americans and Africans in this confrontation, these facts can be placed in some category, or hung on some peg, and are therefore easier to remember. Think, for example, of how you would remember the following facts: names such as Mansa Musa, Elizabeth I, and Incas; dates or periods such as "pre-Columbian," Renaissance, and 1492; places such as Cahokia, Venice, and Mali; and terms such as *matrilineal*, *reciprocal obligation*, and *Black Death*.

Once the facts are mastered within the context of the major themes, you are able to work with, or use, both facts and concepts in a more sophisticated way than just repeating or listing them. You could, for example, contrast the three worlds according to their differing values and beliefs about nature, religion, family, and political and economic goals. Or you could analyze the reasons for the conflict between Spain and England. Or you could apply or transfer your knowledge to similar situations, like the intermingling and conflicts today, perhaps even in your own community, among ethnic and racial groups with differing sets of values. Or you might evaluate how people thought and felt about the effects of the clash of cultures in both the seventeenth and twentieth centuries. Being able to form judgments like these is the highest level of learning and depends upon a prior understanding of specific facts and thematic concepts.

Finally, to check how well you have learned the material of a chapter, it is good to be tested—on both the specific facts and the larger themes of that chapter. This feedback is necessary both to confirm your confidence in how much has been learned and to identify areas that need further study.

To summarize, most people learn best by moving through the following sequence:

1. Engagement in a human story
2. An overview of major themes and concepts
3. Mastery of specific facts that support or illustrate those themes
4. Analysis, synthesis, comparison, application, and evaluation of the themes
5. An opportunity to demonstrate knowledge practicing these steps on tests and other assignments

Each chapter in *The American People* can be understood better by studying it in terms of this basic learning pattern.

HOW TO USE THE STUDY GUIDE WITH THE TEXT

The Study Guide also follows this pattern. Students who work back and forth from the chapter in *The American People* to the chapter in the Guide will continually be reinforcing and strengthening their mastery and enjoyment of American history. With a little experimenting, students will find that it is sometimes better to read the textbook chapter before looking at the Guide and sometimes better to read the Guide before the textbook. We have also included PART summaries and the accounts of three important technological innovations to enhance your learning.

Each chapter contains the following sections:

(1) Chapter Outline (with opening anecdote)

It is helpful to look through the outline before reading a chapter in order to see at a glance both the major topics to be covered and the chapter's organization. The short summary of the human story or anecdote that begins each chapter should point toward these topics and suggest the structure.

(2) Significant Themes and Highlights

Three or four statements will provide an overview summary of the main themes, concepts, threads, major ideas, and special features of each chapter. To consult this section before reading the chapter may be the most helpful thing you can do in order to have some handles or pegs to help you understand and place the many particular facts encountered in the chapter. Keeping these major concepts in mind as you read will prevent you from getting lost in a sea of facts. Specific facts are valuable to a historian only as illustrations of some larger theme. If you have a strong sense of the themes you will more easily remember the appropriate illustrative factual examples when taking examinations.

(3) Learning Goals of the Chapter

The list of the goals, or objectives, of each chapter is a way of providing a self-check on how well you are mastering the material. After completing a chapter, try answering each item. If you can, you are ready to move on. If you cannot, you know which topics to review in the chapter. When you are preparing for examinations, reread the sections on learning goals for the appropriate chapters.

The first 5—6 learning goals indicate the "basic knowledge" you should be familiar with—the essential facts every history student has to know before doing anything else. Such knowledge is usually tested with short-answer exam questions: multiple-choice, true-or-false, identification, fill-in-the-blanks, and similar formats. You also need to know these facts in order to handle more difficult kinds of questions. The second part of the learning goals section includes three goals intended to give you "Practice in Historical Thinking Skills," higher order learning tasks such as analyzing, comparing and contrasting, applying, assessing, and evaluating historical phenomena. This is what we mean by interpretation. These intellectual skills are usually tested by essay questions and paper assignments. You can prepare for these by writing short practice essays on these three learning goals.

(4) Important Dates and Names to Know

Nothing drives history students crazier than having to memorize dates. Yet chronology—the order and sequence of past events—is essential to understanding history. What is most important for students to remember is not that they must memorize every exact date but rather that they should form a general idea of the sequence in which events happened. Remembering key dates is not as mysterious as students often think: it is usually just a matter of common sense. One could, for example, remember that the Declaration of Independence was signed in 1776 and the Constitution in 1787, but what is really important is to get them in the right order. Imagine how silly it would be to reverse them. It is common sense that the bonds of one government had to be dissolved before a new one could be created. The chronologies of important dates will usually include important names to remember as well. Names that are not associated with a particular date but are nevertheless significant are listed at the end of the chronology.

(5) Glossary of Important Terms

Although history is not nearly as filled with jargon and special vocabularies as other disciplines, various unfamiliar terms inevitably turn up in every chapter. These are listed and briefly identified in this section. Remember that your teachers may also have favorite terms that they want you to learn, so it is a good idea to add them to these lists.

(6) Enrichment Ideas

We think this is the most important section in the Guides. In this part is a list of activities and assignments designed to aid and enhance learning of the important themes and concepts in each chapter. Some are activities you can follow and do on your own. A longer list, not included in the Student Guide, contains assignments and classroom activities your instructor may want to use. The variety of suggested approaches to enrich learning—both in the classroom and out—is extensive, but they always begin with further ways of using the "Recovering the Past" feature. This section, found in each chapter, is intended to introduce students of history to the many sources and ways in which historians find out what happened in the past.

A century ago, most historians would probably have said that they recovered the past by reading old manuscripts, primarily government and other institutional documents housed in official archives, and by consulting the letters, papers, and manuscripts of former presidents, senators, generals, and other leaders. But in recent years, as historians have broadened their interest from political and military history (unkindly called "drum and trumpets" history) to include the social history of ordinary people, they have also widened the kinds of sources they find useful in recovering the past. To written government documents and archival manuscripts historians have added private diaries, popular songs, paintings, cartoons, census returns, tax and inventory lists, films and photographs, material objects, oral history, and many other means of recovering the past.

The "RTPs," as the authors affectionately call them, are intended not only to enrich your learning of American history but also to show you how you can become your own historian. For the most part, each means of recovering the past is appropriate to the content of the chapter in which it is found. Thus the work of archaeologists and the contributions archaeology makes to understanding earlier civilizations are discussed in Chapter 1; folktales in the chapter on slavery; and films, oral history, and television in the twentieth-century chapters. Additional ways of recovering the past, such as popular Hollywood feature films and trips to historical areas, are mentioned in the appropriate Enrichment sections in this Study Guide.

(7) Sample Test and Examination Questions

Many students will find this section most useful in preparing for examinations, not because their teachers will necessarily select test questions from those included (though they might) but because students can check for themselves how well they have learned the material in a chapter. Note that the sample questions begin with short-answer types (multiple choice, matching, etc.) to test basic knowledge (how well you remember the material), whereas the later questions are essays and interpretive questions that test historical thinking skills (how well you can compare and contrast, analyze, interpret, apply, and evaluate the main ideas of the chapter). In these higher order questions, you gain practice in learning how to think like historians, doing the kind of basic detective groundwork interpreting evidence from various sources and writing analytic essays.

The test questions for some chapters in this Guide end with a map question, which is a lower-order but fundamentally important content knowledge skill (knowing where places are). Other chapters end with a quotation, chart, or other verbal or quantitative illustration, which we ask you to identify and interpret—who, what, where, when, and why significant. This is a more sophisticated exercise in the detection and interpretation of a historical source.

HOW TO UNDERLINE A CHAPTER

One of the first problems students face when they begin reading a textbook is how much to underline or highlight. A consideration of the purpose of underlining may help guide you through a chapter. The major goal, of course, is to aid memory and comprehension by highlighting the main themes, selecting important examples for each major idea. This helps not only to understand the chapter but also to review for examinations. Too little underlining means that you may end up rereading the entire chapter the night before a test. Too much, in which no discrimination has taken place, may also mean having to reread everything. It is, of course, important to note the topic sentences for each paragraph.

The following is an example of how we would underline a short section from Chapter 1.

Contrasting Worldviews

Having evolved in complete isolation from each other, European and Native American cultures exhibited a wide difference in values. Colonizing Europeans called themselves "civilized" and typically described the people they met in the Americas as "savage," "heathen," or "barbarian." Lurking behind the physical confrontation that took place when Europeans and Native Americans met <u>were latent conflicts over humans' relationship to the environment, the meaning of property, and personal identity.</u>

<u>Europeans</u> and Native Americans conceptualized their relationship to nature in starkly different ways. Regarding the <u>earth as filled with resources for humans to use and exploit</u> for their own benefit, Europeans separated the secular and sacred parts of life, and they placed their own relationships to the natural environment mostly in the secular sphere. <u>Native Americans</u>, however, did not distinguish between the secular and the sacred. For them, <u>every aspect of the natural world was sacred, inhabited by a variety of "beings," each pulsating with spiritual power</u> and all linked together to form a sacred whole. Consequently, if one offended the land by stripping it of its cover, the spiritual power in the land—called "manitou" by some eastern woodland tribes—would strike back. If one overfished or destroyed game beyond one's needs, the spirit forces in fish or animals would take revenge, because humans had broken the mutual trust and <u>reciprocity that governed relations between all beings—human or nonhuman.</u> To neglect reciprocal obligations in nature's domain was to court sickness, hunger, injury, or death.

<u>Europeans</u> believed that <u>land,</u> as a privately held commodity, <u>was a resource to be exploited for human gain.</u> They took for granted property lines, inheritance of land, and courts to settle resulting land disputes. Property was the basis not only of sustenance but also of independence, wealth, status, political rights, and identity. <u>The social structure directly mirrored patterns of land ownership,</u> with a land-wealthy elite at the apex of the social pyramid and a propertyless mass a the bottom.

<u>Native Americans</u> also had concepts of property and boundaries. But they believed that <u>land had sacred qualities and should be held in common.</u> As one German missionary explained the Native American view in the eighteenth century, the Creator "made the Earth and all that it contains for the <u>common good of mankind.</u> Whatever liveth on the land, whatsoever groweth out of the earth, and all that is in the rivers and waters . . . was given jointly to all and everyone is entitled to his share."

<u>Communal ownership sharply limited social stratification and increased a sense of sharing in most Native American communities,</u> much to the amazement of Europeans accustomed to wide disparities of wealth. Not all Europeans were acquisitive, competitive individuals. The majority were peasant farmers living from the soil, living in kin-centered villages with little contact with the outside world, and exchanging goods and labor through barter. <u>But in Europe's cities a wealth-conscious, ambitious individual</u> who valued and sought wider choices and greater opportunities to enhance personal status was coming to the fore. In contrast, <u>Native American traditions stressed the group rather than the individual</u> and <u>valor rather than wealth.</u>

There were <u>exceptions.</u> The empire of the <u>Aztec</u> in Central America and the <u>Inca</u> in South America were <u>highly developed, populous, and stratified.</u> So, in North America, were a few tribes such as the Natchez. But on the eastern and western coasts of the continent and in the Southwest—the regions of contact in the sixteenth and seventeenth centuries—the European newcomers encountered a people whose cultural values differed strikingly from theirs.

European colonizers in North America also found disturbing the <u>matrilineal organization of many tribal societies</u> contrary to the European male-dominated sexual hierarchy. Family membership among most tribes was determined through the <u>female line</u> and divorce was the woman's prerogative. Clans were composed of several matrilineal kin groups related by a blood connection on the mother's side.

8

PART ONE (Chapters 1–5)

A COLONIZING PEOPLE 1492–1776

America has always been a nation of immigrants, an elaborate cultural mosaic created out of the unending streams of people who, for four centuries, have flocked to its shores from every corner of the world. It is the colonial roots of this intermingling of people and cultures that provide an organizing framework for the first part of this book. America began with the convergence of people from the three continents of North America, Europe, and Africa.

Chapter 1, "Ancient America and Africa," explores the mingling of their values, institutions, and lifeways during the fifteenth and sixteenth centuries. Insights to African, European, and Native American life and culture prior to contact are revealed. Chapter 2, "Europeans and Africans Reach the Americas," examines Spanish conquest of the Americas, the early African slave trade, and the blending of cultures in the Americas. Chapter 3, "Colonizing a Continent in the Seventeenth Century," explores six regions of settlement along the Atlantic seaboard and the Caribbean. The interplay of religious idealism, economic opportunity, political experimentation, and social adaptation to the new environment is examined on the Chesapeake tobacco coast; in Puritan New England; in the French, Dutch, and English colonies from the St. Lawrence to the Hudson rivers; in proprietary Carolina; in Quaker Pennsylvania; and New Spain's Northern Frontier.

The ability to grow from small and struggling settlements in the seventeenth century to thriving, more populous colonies in the early eighteenth century depended above all on exploiting the natural resources of North America. Chapter 4, "The Maturing of Colonial Society," traces the development of the colonies of England, Spain, and France in the first half of the eighteenth century. It stresses the increasingly complex, yet unfinished, character of colonial society, highlights its regional differences, and shows how economic growth, religious revival, and political maturation prepared the English colonists by 1750 for the epic events that would occur in the next generation. It was this fluidity of colonial society that made the Seven Years' War (1756 - 1763) and the subsequent coming of the American Revolution such a multifaceted and dynamic period, as Chapter 5, "The Strains of Empire," spells out. Many other "American revolutions" will follow in our history.

1

Ancient America and Africa

(1) CHAPTER OUTLINE

As the stories about four important women of this era demonstrate, deep transformations were underway in West Africa, in southern and western Europe, and in the Americas. The cultures of Africa, Europe, and the Americas prior to contact are revealed.

The Peoples of America Before Columbus
    Migration to the Americas
    Hunters, Farmers, and Environmental Factors
    Mesoamerican Empires
    Regional North American Cultures
    The Iroquois
    Pre-Contact Population
    Contrasting Worldviews

Africa on the Eve of Contact
    The Spread of Islam
    The Kingdoms of Central and West Africa
    African Slavery
    The African Ethos

Europe on the Eve of Invading the Americas
    The Rebirth of Europe
    The New Monarchies and the Expansionist Impulse

Conclusion: The Approach of a New Global Age

(2) SIGNIFICANT THEMES AND HIGHLIGHTS

1. The clash that developed when the people of three continents—North America, Europe, and Africa—began to encounter each other forms the opening chapter of American history and is therefore the opening chapter of the textbook. With the stories of Isabella of Castile, Tecuichpotzin, Elizabeth I of England, and Queen Njinga, we see the intermingling and transformation of three worlds.

2. The chapter challenges the concept that Africans and Native Americans were passive primitive bystanders awaiting conquest. Native American, Africans, and Europeans were all critical participants in the making of the modern world.

3. The spread of Islam and the rise of great empires in West and Central Africa is also examined.

4. By taking readers inside the cultural beliefs and experiences of Native Americans and Africans, as well as Europeans, this chapter serves to counteract the traditional ethnocentric view that sees all developments through the eyes of Europeans. An example of this is the oft-repeated phrase "Columbus discovered America," implying that there was no life or culture in the Americas until a European found it in 1492.

(3) LEARNING GOALS

Familiarity with Basic Knowledge

After reading this chapter, you should be able to:

1. Locate and briefly describe the Native American Mound Builders of the Ohio and Mississippi River valleys, the Pueblo dwellers of the Southwest, and the Iroquois Indians of the East Coast.

2. Describe Native American attitudes toward and beliefs about the natural world, wealth, community, family, and men and women.

3. Name and locate three West African kingdoms between the fifth and fourteenth centuries and describe West African beliefs about family, religion, and social organization.

4. Explain the political, economic, and religious changes in early modern Europe that led to the exploration and eventual settlement of North America.

5. Explain the navigational improvements that led to European exploration.

Practice in Historical Thinking Skills

After reading this chapter, you should be able to:

1. Compare and contrast the values and lifestyles of the three worlds—Native American, African, and European—that met in the Americas early in the sixteenth century.

2. Evaluate the outcomes of that collision for each world. What do you think and feel about these outcomes?

3. Evaluate the motivations for European exploration. What do you think about their motivations?

(4) IMPORTANT DATES AND NAMES TO KNOW

Pre-Columbian epochs:

35,000 B.C.E.	First humans cross Bering Land Bridge to reach the Americas
12,000 B.C.E.	Beringian epoch ends
8000 B.C.E.	Paleo-Indian phase ends
500 B.C.E.	Archaic era ends
500 B.C.E.-1000 C.E.	Post-Archaic era in North America
600 C.E.-1100	Rise of mound building center at Cahokia
632-750	Islamic conquest of North Africa spreads Muslim faith
800-1026	Kingdom of Ghana controls West Africa's trade
1000	Norse seafarers establish settlements in Newfoundland Kingdom of Benin develops
1000-1500	Kingdoms of Ghana, Mali, Songhai in Africa
1200s	Pueblo societies develop village life in southwestern North America
1235	Defeating the Ghanaian king, Mali becomes a West African power
1291	Marco Polo's return from East Asia to Venice quickens European trade with Eastern Hemisphere

1300s	Rise of Aztec society in Valley of Mexico
1300-1450	Italian Renaissance
1324	Mansa Musa's pilgrimage to Mecca expands Muslim influence in West Africa
1420s	Portuguese sailors explore west coast of Africa
1435	Kingdom of Songhai declares independence from Kingdom of Mali
1450-1600	Northern European Renaissance
1460s-1590s	Kingdom of Songhai controls West Africa's trading societies
1469	Marriage of Castile's Isabella and Aragon's Ferdinand creates Spain
1500s	Quickening of western European trade and production of consumer goods

Other Names to Know

Prince Henry the Navigator	Mansa Musa	Marco Polo
	Ghana	Iroquois
Isabella of Castile	Magna Carta	Cahokia

(5) GLOSSARY OF IMPORTANT TERMS

matrilineal: tracing descent and property and political rights through the mother

Mesoamerica: the middle region bridging the great land masses of South and North America

Muslim: a person believing in the religion of Islam, which began in the seventh century and spread throughout the Middle East and northern Africa and eventually to Asia and Europe in succeeding centuries (Muslims, or Moslems, were sometimes called Moors by Europeans)

Pre-Columbian era: the period of history before Columbus in which Native American Indian cultures lived in the Americas undiscovered—and unaffected—by Europeans

Renaissance: period of cultural rebirth in Europe (fifteenth-sixteenth centuries)

(6) ENRICHMENT IDEAS

1. Find out which Native American tribes and nations lived in your part of the country and whether there are any archaeological working sites or remains, like Cahokia, to visit. Also visit any museums or historical parks that feature local Indian history.

2. Assume that you are an archaeologist or anthropologist who wants to understand and reconstruct in your region as much of the original Indian culture and typical daily life as possible from relics and other remains. Present your findings to others in various forms: oral report, written paper, table display showing artifacts and a model of Indian life, or artistic drawings or skits illustrating Indian culture.

3. Pretend that you are an archaeologist or anthropologist from some distant future who wants to understand and reconstruct as much as possible of present-day culture and daily life in your community. Imagine the absolute destruction of all written records and the near-destruction and burying under dirt and debris of material objects and structures. As you dig up the remains or observe unusual topological and other features (like dammed-up streams, terraced and flattened hills, or roadway patterns), how much of the original daily life and culture do you think you could reconstruct?

4. Imagine yourself as an alien, who has never seen earthlings, arriving to explore and settle the planet Earth. From the behavior of human beings, what kind of conclusions might you draw about their cultural patterns and values? What images do you have about groups different from your own? Think about both positive and negative images.

5. Look over the opening anecdote. Imagine yourself as each of the four women leaders, write a diary entry discussing the specific challenges you face as the leader of your specific group.

(7) SAMPLE TEST AND EXAMINATION QUESTIONS

Multiple choice: Choose the best answer.

1. The "New World" was first entered by people from what is now Asia
    a. around 35,000 B.C.E.
    b. about 14,000 to 25,000 years ago.
    c. in about 1000 C.E.
    d. in 1492.

2. The five tribes that comprised the League of the Iroquois were
    a. Cahokia, Hopi, Zuni, Pueblo, and Mohawks.
    b. Aztec, Olmec, Toltec, Inca, and Mayan.
    c. Choctaw, Chickasaws, Cherokee, Creeks, and Seminoles.
    d. Mohawk, Oneidas, Onondagas, Cayugas, and Senecas.

3. Cahokia was the center of
   a. "Hopewell" culture.
   b. "Mississippi" culture.
   c. "Pueblo" culture.
   d. "Iroquois" culture.

4. According to Native Americans, before the European invasion
   a. the natural world was a resource given by a Christian God.
   b. every part of the natural environment was sacred.
   c. the belief that spirits resided in nature was fading.
   d. land was the basis of status and identity.

5. From the fifth to the fourteenth centuries, West Africa
   a. was a savage land of nomadic hunters.
   b. was colonized and exploited by various European nations.
   c. was engaged in perpetual warfare with Muslims from the Middle East.
   d. featured the development of a series of kingdoms with relatively advanced cultures and complex political structures.

6. In the fifteenth century, West African societies
   a. developed an extensive industrial system based on slaves captured in tribal wars.
   b. had the most brutal system of slavery in the civilized world.
   c. respected the privileges of education and marriage and the protection of the law for slaves.
   d. provided legal protection and rights only for slave children.

7. Each of these was a West African empire EXCEPT
   a. Ghana.   c. Songhai.
   b. Mali.   d. Egypt.

8. By the end of the fifteenth century a new political entity, _____, had arisen in European countries like Portugal.
   a. dictatorships   b. feudal states
   c. nation-states   d. democracies

9. In traditional African slavery
   a. slaves were considered chattel.
   b. slavery was race based.
   c. status of a slave was limited and not inherited by offspring.
   d. the primary occupation of slaves was gang field worker.

10. The Magna Carta
    a. curbed the powers of the monarchy and established the parliament in England.
    b. authorized Christopher Columbus' first expedition to the Americas.
    c. created a parliament solely composed of hereditary members.
    d. was a kingdom in Central Africa.

11. The Renaissance that encouraged innovation in science and the arts in Europe peaked in
    a. the time from 500 -1000 B.C.E.   c. the late fifteenth century.
    b. the centuries before 1400.   d. the late sixteenth century.

12. All of the following changes in fifteenth century Europe led to an expansionist impulse EXCEPT
    a. the rise of new monarchies.
    b. technological improvements.
    c. the rise of the Protestant denomination.
    d. trade rivalry with the Muslims.

13. Which of the following pairs is not correct?
    a. Tecuichpotzin : Aztec.   b. Queen Njinga : Angola.
    c. Elizabeth I : France.   d. Queen Isabella : Spain.

14. The expansionist impulse of European monarchs in the latter fifteenth century was
    a. temporarily subdued by the growth of the Renaissance culture.
    b. nourished by population decline and civil disorder.
    c. disrupted by internal wars of bickering nobles.
    d. motivated by a desire to bypass Muslim merchants in trade with Africa and Asia.

15. Which of the following nations became the early leader of the transatlantic slave trade and European exploration?
    a. Spain.   b. Portugal.
    c. Holland.   d. France.

Essays

1. Compare and contrast African, Native American, and European beliefs and practices about the natural world, status of women, property and wealth, and community and family life.

2. Discuss the differences between traditional African slavery and transatlantic slavery.

3. Analyze European motivations for exploring and eventually settling the New World.

4. "Too often in historical writing, Europeans reaching the Americas are portrayed as the carriers of a superior culture that inevitably vanquished people living in a primitive if not 'savage' state." Selecting appropriate evidence from the chapter, write an essay refuting this depiction of Africans and Native Americans as a passive or primitive people.

2

Europeans and Africans Reach the Americas

(1) CHAPTER OUTLINE

Between 1492 and 1504 we see people like Estevan and Alvar Cabeza de Vaca brought together from three previously unconnected continents. This chapter examines the Columbian voyages, the arrival of the Spanish conquistadors and their conquest of Mesoamerica and the southern regions of North America. A central theme is the exchange of goods and cultures between Europe, Africa, and the Americas that begin to create the modern world.

Breaching the Atlantic
> The Columbian Voyages
> Religious Conflict During the Era of Reconnaissance

The Spanish Conquest of America
> Caribbean Experiments
> The Conquistadors' Onslaught at Tenochtitlán
> The Great Dying
> The Columbian Exchange
> Silver, Sugar, and Their Consequences
> Spain's Northern Frontier

England Looks West
> England Challenges Spain
> The Westward Fever
> Anticipating North America

African Bondage
> The Slave Trade
> The Middle Passage
> Slavery in Early Spanish Colonies

Conclusion: Converging Worlds

(2) SIGNIFICANT THEMES AND HIGHLIGHTS

1. The clash of three cultures from three continents—the Americas, Europe, and Africa—affects tremendously the cultures on each continent. It is the basis for conflict and community for the next five hundred years.

2. A secondary clash within the European white world, that between Catholic Spain and Protestant England, explains the different development of Spanish Central and South America and English North America.

3. By taking readers inside the cultural beliefs and experiences of Native Americans and Africans, as well as Europeans, this chapter serves to counteract the traditional ethnocentric view that sees all developments through the eyes of Europeans. An example of this is the oft-repeated phrase "Columbus discovered America," implying that there was no life or culture in the Americas until a European found it in 1492.

(3) LEARNING GOALS

Familiarity with Basic Knowledge

After reading this chapter, you should be able to:

1. Explain the political, economic, and religious changes in early modern Europe that led to the exploration and eventual settlement of North America.

2. Locate on a map the names and routes of the most significant Spanish, English, French, and Dutch explorers and conquerors in the fifteenth and sixteenth centuries.

3. Describe the impact of the European conquest of the Americas on the Native American Indian population.

4. Explain the economic impact of exploration on the European continent.

5. Explain African participation in the transatlantic slave trade.

6. Describe the conditions of the Middle Passage.

7. Locate on a map the areas European slave traders carried the majority of enslaved Africans during the fifteenth and sixteenth centuries.

Practice in Historical Thinking Skills

After reading this chapter, you should be able to:

1. Evaluate the outcomes that resulted from the collision between Europe, the Americas, and Africa. What do you think and feel about these outcomes?

2. Compare and contrast the cultures of Spain and England, and their motivations for settling the Americas.

3. Explain the images that Europeans had of the Native American and African populations. How were the realities different from the perceptions?

4. Analyze the Islamic and transatlantic slave trade.

(4) IMPORTANT DATES AND NAMES TO KNOW

1440s	Portuguese begin kidnapping Africans and trading with them for slaves on Africa's western coast
1460s	Using African labor, sugar plantations in Portuguese Madeira become major exporters
1492	Christopher Columbus lands on Caribbean islands Spanish expel Moors (Muslims) and Jews
1493-1504	Columbus makes three additional voyages to the Americas
1493	Spain plants first colony in Americas on Hispaniola
1494	Treaty of Tordesillas
1497-1585	French and English explore northern part of the Americas
1498	Vasco da Gama reaches India after sailing around Africa
Early 1500s	First Africans reach the Americas with Spanish
1508-1511	Spanish conquistadors subjugate native people on Puerto Rico and Cuba
1513	Portuguese explorers reach China
1517	Luther attacks Catholicism and begins Protestant Reformation
1520	First disease contracted from Spanish devastates Aztec people
1521	Cortés conquers the Aztecs

1528	Spain plants first settlement on Florida coast
1527-1536	Cabeza de Vaca *entrada* across southern region of North America
1530s	Calvin calls for religious reform
1533	Pizarro conquers the Incas
1534	Church of England established
1539-1542	De Soto expedition explores the southeast
1540-1542	Coronado explores the Southwest
1558	Elizabeth I crowned Queen of England
1585	English plant settlement on Roanoke Island
1588	English defeat the Spanish Armada
1590	Roanoke settlement fails
1603	James I succeeds Elizabeth I

Other Names to Know

Bartolemé de Las Casas	Thomas Hariot	Francis Drake
Estevan (Estanvanico)	John White	King Philip II
Moctezuma II	Francisco Feliz de Sousa	

(5) GLOSSARY OF IMPORTANT TERMS

Columbian Exchange: most significant geographical rearrangement of plant and animal life between Europe and the Americas with profound environmental and human consequences

conquistador: any of the sixteenth century Spanish conquerors of Mexico, Peru, etc.

Middle Passage: the journey during the transatlantic slave trade from Africa to the Americas and Europe

Moors: any of a Muslim people living chiefly in Northwest Africa

Protestant Reformation: period in Europe in the sixteenth century of protest against the Roman Catholic church and the creation of new (Protestant) religious institutions

(6) ENRICHMENT IDEAS

1. Imagine that you are an enslaved African, one of the European explorers, or a Native American during the fifteenth and sixteenth century. Write a journal entry describing your contact with people of another land and culture. What might be some obstacles in interacting with people of another culture? What might be some positive outcomes of contact?

2. Find an old history textbook that discusses European exploration during the fifteenth and sixteenth century. Compare and contrast the interpretation of the old history textbook with your current one. How do historical interpretations change over time?

3. Pretend that you are a Catholic priest living during the time of the Protestant Reformation. Write a letter to your parishioners explaining some of the difference in doctrine between Protestants and Catholics. How would you respond to some of the criticisms against the Catholic Church? Do a similar exercise from the perspective of a Protestant minister. How would you respond to criticisms against the Protestant Church?

4. Create a poster illustrating the Columbian Exchange. Use the "Analyzing History" inset to guide your project.

5. Imagine yourself as a newly enslaved African. Write a letter to people back home explaining how you were acquired and what has happened to your life since your capture.

(7) SAMPLE TEST AND EXAMINATION QUESTIONS

Multiple choice: Choose the best answer.

1. In the latter half of the fifteenth century, Christopher Columbus
    a. received financial backing by Prince Henry the Navigator for a westward voyage.
    b. overestimated the distance between Europe and Japan.
    c. argued that Europeans could reach the Indies by sailing west rather than east.
    d. reaped significant fame and riches from his four voyages of exploration.

2. According to Martin Luther
    a. only a chosen few deserved salvation.
    b. salvation came through faith in God's grace.
    c. only non-Catholics could ever be saved.
    d. salvation was earned through good works.

3. The doctrines of Protestant leader John Calvin
    a. offered a system for both self-discipline and social control.
    b. emphasized the need for hierarchical church structure.
    c. offered hope of salvation to most believers.
    d. appealed only to the poorest and most oppressed peoples of Europe.

4. The Treaty of Tordesillas divided settlement of the Americas between
   a. Spain and Portugal.
   b. Spain and England.
   c. Spain and France.
   d. France and England.

5. The population of the Americas dramatically declined following the arrival of Europeans primarily because of the
   a. enslavement of Native Americans by Europeans.
   b. lack of immunity among Native Americans to European diseases.
   c. loss of morale and sense of hopelessness that pervaded Native American societies.
   d. policy of systematic genocide employed by European explorers toward Native Americans.

6. Which of the following pairs is not correct?
   a. Pizzaro : Incas.
   b. Cortes : Aztecs.
   c. de Soto : New Mexico and Arizona.
   d. Ponce de Leon : Florida.

7. What percentage (estimated) of the inhabitants of the Americas died of diseases brought by Europeans?
   a. 25 percent.
   b. 67 percent.
   c. 75 percent.
   d. 95 percent.

8. Motivation(s) for Spanish settlement included
   a. spread of the Catholic religion.
   b. national pride.
   c. dreams of personal enrichment.
   d. all of the above.

9. The massive flow of silver bullion from the Americas to Europe in the sixteenth and seventeenth centuries
   a. triggered a sharp increase in the price of goods.
   b. delayed further exploration of America.
   c. increased prevailing wage rates in Europe.
   d. hampered capitalist modes of production.

10. The primary enterprise of the Portuguese in Brazil during the late sixteenth and early seventeenth centuries involved the
    a. extraction of silver.
    b. enslavement of Native American laborers.
    c. conversion of Native Americans to Catholicism.
    d. production of sugar.

11. Which of the following best describes England's motivations for moving westward to North America?
    a. They only wanted to expand their fishing capabilities.
    b. The quest for gold and silver.
    c. Rivalry with Spain, a quest for new markets, and an expanding population.
    d. The desire to Christianize heathen Indians.

12. The defeat of the Spanish Armada by England in 1588
   a. solidified Catholicism in England.
   b. decreased nationalistic spirit in England.
   c. increased English interest in overseas exploration and colonization.
   d. brought about continued European religious wars.

13. Early European images of the "New World"
   a. described an earthly paradise full of riches.
   b. depicted a harsh environment, not conducive to farming.
   c. pictured only backward, hostile savages.
   d. described all of the above.

14. English colonizing ventures in the New World differed from earlier Portuguese and Spanish efforts in that English attempts were
   a. immediate and major successes.
   b. met with little or no Native American resistance.
   c. strictly coordinated and governed by the Crown.
   d. privately owned and financed.

15. The least likely destination of European slave traders in the seventeenth century would have been
   a. the West Indies.   b. Brazil.
   c. North America.   d. Spanish America.

Essays

1. Discuss the various explorers and the areas that they conquered. Examine the process of how these areas were dominated. Discuss the reaction of the Native American and/or the African. What steps, if any, did they take against colonization?

2. Analyze English motivations for exploring and eventually settling the New World. Compare and contrast their motives with those of the Spanish.

3. Evaluate the converging of three worlds—Native American, African, and European—in the Americas. What was gained and what was lost by each of the three?

4. "Neither the Spanish nor the English respected Indian culture and society; this lack of respect enabled them to destroy Native American life with few regrets." Write an essay supporting or rejecting this statement, selecting appropriate evidence.

5. Explain how the religious changes of the Protestant Reformation affected the English colonization of America.

6. Explain the transatlantic slave trade from acquisition in Africa until their new lives in the Americas. Why do you think the Islamic slave trade in northern Africa has received less attention than the transatlantic slave trade?

3

Colonizing a Continent in the Seventeenth Century

(1) CHAPTER OUTLINE

Anthony and Mary Johnson, two freed slaves, live in the uneasy world between freedom and slavery. Their experiences are just one of thousands detailing the experiences of seventeenth-century immigrants who arrived in North America. Free immigrants, indentured servants from Europe, the African labor force, and Native Americans had to learn to cope with new environments, new social situations, and new mixings of people in the six areas of early colonization.

The Chesapeake Tobacco Coast
    Jamestown, Sot Weed and Indentured Servants
    Expansion and Indian War
    Proprietary Maryland
    Daily Life on the Chesapeake
    Bacon's Rebellion Engulfs Virginia
    The Southern Transition to Slave Labor
    The System of Bondage

Massachusetts and Its Offspring
    Puritanism in England
    Puritan Predecessors in New England
    Errand into the Wilderness
    New Englanders and Indians
    The Web of Village Life
    King Philip's War in New England
    Slavery in New England

From the St. Lawrence to the Hudson
    France's America
    England Challenges the Dutch

Proprietary Carolina: A Restoration Reward
    The Indian Debacle
    Early Carolina Society

The Quakers' Peaceable Kingdom
The Early Friends
Early Quaker Designs
Pacifism in a Militant World: Quakers and Native Americans
Building the Peaceable Kingdom
The Limits of Perfectionism

New Spain's Northern Frontier
Popé's Revolt
Decline of Florida's Missions

An Era of Instability
Organizing the Empire
The Glorious Revolution in North America
The Social Basis of Politics
Witchcraft in Salem

Conclusion: The Achievement of New Societies

(2) SIGNIFICANT THEMES AND HIGHLIGHTS

1. A theme running throughout the chapter, illustrated by King Philip's War and Bacon's Rebellion, is the confrontation in North America between two cultures: the English colonists (in various kinds of settlements) and Native American tribes. The two cultures collided as the colonists sought to realize the goals that had lured them to the New World and the Indians sought to defend their tribal homelands.

2. A second theme focuses on tensions growing out of the religious and economic motivations behind settlement. Many English colonists came to America to create religious utopias, a New World Zion. Others, even in the same settlement, came for economic opportunity, gold, and land. Regardless of motive, the colonists experienced limits to their aspirations: both utopia and economic opportunity proved elusive, the former far more than the latter.

3. Another recurrent theme of the chapter is the tension between religious idealism and violence. The colonial world was a violent one, both in contact with the Native Americans and in the social conflicts that emerged in the difficult early years of settlement.

4. The English colonists not only clashed with Native American cultures but also developed different cultures themselves. This chapter is structured around the reconstruction of the modes of settlement and character of life in five distinctly different societies along the Atlantic Coast: the Chesapeake region of Virginia and Maryland, Puritan New England, New York under the Dutch and English, proprietary Carolina, and Quaker Pennsylvania.

In the account of each society is a picture of daily life as reflected in the architecture of houses, material household belongings, patterns of family life, and the role of women.

5. Small insurrections against colonial administrators and elites, triggered by the Glorious Revolution of 1688, erupted in several colonies. Although they were in no way a "dress rehearsal" for the American Revolution, they did reveal some of the social and political tensions growing out of the attempt to plant English society in the New World.

(3) LEARNING GOALS

Familiarity with Basic Knowledge

After reading this chapter, you should be able to:

1. Locate the various distinct settlements on a map of the Atlantic Coast, in particular Jamestown and the Chesapeake Bay tobacco area, Roanoke Island, Charleston, Plymouth, Boston and Massachusetts Bay, New York, the Hudson River, Delaware, the Connecticut and James rivers, and Philadelphia and the greater Pennsylvania settlement.

2. Describe the changing population, social patterns, and daily life of the Chesapeake tobacco coast in the seventeenth century.

3. Describe the beliefs, social patterns, and character of village life of the New England Puritans in England in early seventeenth-century Massachusetts.

4. Describe the course and consequences of King Philip's War in New England and Bacon's Rebellion in Virginia.

5. Outline the major features of economic and social life in seventeenth-century New York and Carolina.

6. Describe Quaker beliefs and the efforts to build a peaceable kingdom in William Penn's settlement in Pennsylvania.

7. Discuss Spanish missionary activity in Florida and New Mexico and its impact on settlement activity in the United States.

8. Explain the key ideas England used to organize its empire. How was control affected by the Glorious Revolution?

Practice in Historical Thinking Skills

After reading this chapter, you should be able to:

1. Compare and contrast the reasons and motivations for the settlement of each of the five main colonies, and describe the relationship of each of the five settlements with the Native American tribes of that region.

2. Reconstruct and compare the essentials of daily life, including the lives of women, in each of the six settlements in the seventeenth century.

3. Discuss whether you think utopian idealism or economic necessity was a more important motivation in the settlement and development of the English colonies.

4. Show the most important effects of the Glorious Revolution in England and of European national rivalries on the colonies in the late seventeenth and early eighteenth centuries.

(4) IMPORTANT DATES AND NAMES TO KNOW

1607	Jamestown settled
1616-1621	Native American population in New England decimated by European diseases
1617	First tobacco crop shipped from Virginia
1619	First Africans arrive in Jamestown
1620	Pilgrims land at Plymouth
1622	Powhatan tribes attack Virginia settlements
1624	Dutch colonize mouth of Hudson River
1630	Puritan immigration to Massachusetts Bay
1632	Maryland grant to Lord Baltimore
1633-1634	Native Americans in New England again struck by European diseases
1635	Roger Williams banished and flees to Rhode Island
1637	New England wages war against the Pequot Indians
1638	Anne Hutchinson exiled to Rhode Island

1640s	New England merchants enter slave trade Virginia forbids Blacks to carry firearms
1642-1649	English Civil War ends great migration to New England
1643	Confederation of New England
1650-1670	Judicial and legislative decisions in Chesapeake colonies solidify racial lines
1651	Parliament passes first navigation act
1659-1661	Puritans hang three Quaker men and one Quaker woman on Boston Common
1660	Restoration of King Charles II in England
1663	Carolina charter granted to eight proprietors
1664	English capture New Netherland and rename it New York Royal grant of the Jersey lands to proprietors
1673-1685	French expand into Mississippi valley
1675-1677	King Philip's War in New England
1676	Bacon's Rebellion in Virginia
1680	Popé's revolt in New Mexico
1681	William Penn receives Pennsylvania grant
1684	Massachusetts charter recalled
1688	Glorious Revolution in England, followed by accession of William and Mary
1689	Overthrow of Governor Andros in New England Leisler's Rebellion in New York
1690s	Transition from white indentured servitude to black slave labor begins in Chesapeake region
1692	Witchcraft hysteria in Salem

Other Names to Know

Captain John Smith	Anthony Johnson	Metacomet
Samuel de Champlain	William Bradford	Mary Dyer
John Winthrop	Olaudah Equiano	Sir William Berkeley
John Locke	Pocahontas	King James II

(5) GLOSSARY OF IMPORTANT TERMS

antinomianism: an interpretation of Puritan doctrine associated with Anne Hutchinson that stressed mystical elements in God's grace and diverged from orthodox Puritan views on salvation

genocide: the willed extermination of a race or ethnic group by another

Glorious Revolution: the English revolution of 1688 that replaced James II with William and Mary; the revolution was based on the rejection of the "divine right" of kings and was a victory for Protestants, parliamentary power, and the English merchant and gentry class

indentured servants: European migrants, usually young and single, who entered into work contracts for a specified period of years in exchange for free passage to the New World and sometimes a promise of land at the end of the contract

magistrates: secular, civil leaders in Massachusetts Bay, usually not ministers

Pilgrims: a radical separatist group of English Protestants who settled at Plymouth in order to be left alone to lead a pure and primitive life

proprietors: prominent Englishmen to whom the king granted vast areas of land in the New World

Puritans: English Protestants who wished not only to purify the Church of England but also to reform English society; they came to New England to set up a model community as an example to England

Society of Friends (Quakers): a visionary radical sect, much persecuted, whose members believed in, among other things, an inner light that brought them close to God, equality in religious and social life, pacifism, and defiance of authority when it denied their right to practice their religion

(6) ENRICHMENT IDEAS

1. As an extension of the Recovering the Past section in this chapter, recall the differences in housing between Massachusetts Bay and the Chesapeake region. How do the houses and their furnishings show the differences and similarities in the two societies? Find examples of house design in Maryland and Virginia in the early eighteenth century. What are the significant differences between the earlier Chesapeake housing and these? What do the newer designs reveal about social and economic changes? You can also compare the Boardman house to eighteenth-century Massachusetts houses to see what kind of changes have taken place there.

2. Write a letter or diary entry describing the daily life of a typical inhabitant on a typical day in three of the five settlements in seventeenth-century America.

3. Write a will for an individual colonist of the late seventeenth and early eighteenth centuries leaving items that were most likely to exist in an ordinary household.

4. Construct an imaginary document reflecting each settlement's attitude toward and relationship with the area's Indian tribes. The document might be a sermon, a treaty, a leader's policy statement, a letter by a young man or woman in the settlement, or a speech (or letter) by a young Indian of the appropriate area.

5. Chart the main events in Anthony and Mary Johnson's lives and the lives of their children. How might one explain the changing nature of race relations?

6. Imagine yourself to be an indentured servant in the Chesapeake. Were you to write a letter home to a brother or sister, how would you describe your life? Would you encourage your brother or sister to come to the New World?

7. For those near local museums with eighteenth century exhibits, a visit and brief description of items and their significance will enhance understanding of daily life.

(7) SAMPLE TEST AND EXAMINATION QUESTIONS

Multiple choice: Choose the best answer.

1. The Jamestown colony suffered all of the following problems of population EXCEPT
   a. too few skilled workers who had useful talents in a frontier environment.
   b. too many gold-seeking gentlemen.
   c. too many slaves.
   d. too few women.

2. Most indentured servants who came to Virginia and Maryland in the seventeenth century were
   a. married couples.
   b. young, male, and poor.
   c. young, single, and female.
   d. black Africans.

3. Before 1700, houses in the Chesapeake region were
   a. crude, one-room structures.
   b. large homes with sleeping lofts and lean-to kitchens.
   c. small predecessors of plantation-style houses.
   d. connected to long, tobacco-drying barns made of brick.

4. Women in Chesapeake society, as compared to New England,
   a. died young and were scarce.
   b. were given religious freedom.
   c. lived long lives, bearing many children.
   d. were at the center of both economic and political life.

5. Puritans migrated to Massachusetts Bay because they wanted
   a. to convert heathens.
   b. freedom from oppressive government taxes.
   c. to set up an experiment in religious toleration.
   d. to pursue their vision of a pure religious community, free from persecuting authorities.

6. Bacon's Rebellion involved all of the following issues EXCEPT
   a. rivalry between free blacks and indentured servants for land near Williamsburg.
   b. a lack of opportunity for land expansion.
   c. declining tobacco prices and rising taxes, which aggravated social class conflict.
   d. conflict between white frontiersmen and the Susquehannock Indians.

7. The underlying cause of King Philip's War was
   a. the execution of three Wampanoags for murdering an Englishman.
   b. young tribesmen's anger over white encroachment on their lands.
   c. King Philip's desire for an English wife.
   d. all of the above.

8. Roger Williams was a problem for the ruling authorities in Massachusetts Bay because
   a. he advocated mandatory worship, enforced by the government if necessary.
   b. he accused the Puritans of illegal intrusion on Indian lands.
   c. he embraced "coerced religion."
   d. all of the above.

9. Anne Hutchinson was excommunicated from a Boston church primarily because
   a. she challenged traditional religious, political, and social authority.
   b. she spoke against antinomianism.
   c. she opposed wage and price controls.
   d. all of the above.

10. The results of King Philip's War included
    a. the extension of the New England frontier.
    b. the rebuilding of all of New England's 90 towns.
    c. the devastation of Indian society in New England.
    d. the call for colonial unity.

11. Which settlement did King Charles II grant to those that supported him during his exile?
    a. Rhode Island.
    b. Pennsylvania.
    c. Carolina.
    d. Maryland.

12. Quakers believed in all of the following EXCEPT
    a. equality of all persons, including women, in religious matters.
    b. renunciation of the use of force in human affairs.
    c. signing witnesses oaths on the Bible.
    d. no church leaders or institutions standing between an individual and God.

13. Sir Edmund Andros outraged New Englanders by
    a. abolishing freedom of religion.
    b. turning an Anglican church into a Catholic one.
    c. initiating trial by jury.
    d. imposing taxes without legislative consent.

14. In settling Pennsylvania, Quakers sought to
    a. acquire as much Indian land as possible, whatever means necessary.
    b. keep out non-Quakers.
    c. maintain a sense of community based on kinship and a sense of common endeavor.
    d. earn money for the church by selling land at high prices.

15. The Salem witchcraft trials were evidence of
    a. multiple tensions and hysteria growing from community instability.
    b. the Devil's plan to destroy Puritanism.
    c. an Indian plot to avenge white massacres.
    d. the irrationality of teenage girls.

Identify and show a relationship between each of the following pairs:

Virginia	*and*	Massachusetts Bay Company
meetinghouse	*and*	town meeting
Captain John Smith	*and*	Powhatan
Anne Hutchinson	*and*	Roger Williams
Jacob Leisler	*and*	Sir Edmund Andros
John Winthrop	*and*	William Bradford
Nathaniel Bacon	*and*	King Philip

[This question form, which invites a short essay, combines a basic memory task (identifying the person or term) with a higher-order thinking skill (showing a connection). Note that the instruction says "a" relationship, not "the" relationship, suggesting that there is no single "right answer." There are many possible connections, but in the following example each new answer is better than the last: Anne Hutchinson and Roger Williams were both Puritans; they were both Puritans who left Massachusetts Bay; they were both Puritans who left Massachusetts Bay because of religious beliefs; they were both Puritans who left Massachusetts Bay because of religious beliefs that challenged traditional authority.]

Essays

1. Compare and contrast the social patterns of life in the Chesapeake area, New England, and Pennsylvania.

2. The character of immigration to the Chesapeake, Massachusetts Bay, the Carolinas, and Pennsylvania goes a long way toward explaining the social development of each place. Discuss with evidence.

3. Why do you think utopian perfectionism proved to be so elusive for colonial Americans? To what extent do you think the answer is found in human nature or in historical conditions?

4. In what ways does this chapter suggest that racism is a continuing part of American life? Which came first in American society, racism or slavery? What relevance does this chapter have for today? What social or international conflicts still occur between peoples?

Identify and Interpret: Quotation
(that is, state who, what, where, when, and why significant)

We must be knit together in this work as one man. We must entertain each other in brotherly affection. . . . We must delight in each other, make others' conditions our own, rejoice together, mourn together, labor and suffer together: always having before our eyes our commission and community in the work, our community as members of the same body. . . . We shall find that the God of Israel is among us, when ten of us shall be able to resist a thousand of our enemies, when He shall make us a praise and glory, that men shall say of succeeding plantations: "The Lord make it like that of New England." For we must consider that we shall be as a city upon a hill, the eyes of all people are upon us.

4

The Maturing of Colonial Society

(1) CHAPTER OUTLINE

Hannah Cook Heaton was a typical colonial woman: she was married to a farmer, had children, and went to church. After hearing the inspirational preaching of Great Awakening evangelists, Heaton underwent a conversion experience that caused her to reject her present (and husband's) church in favor of an uneducated lay preacher and her own reading of the Bible. Heaton challenged traditional authority by not submitting to her husband, defying local laws requiring church attendance, and questioning the community minister.

The North: A Land of Family Farms
    Northern Agricultural Society
    Unfree Labor
    Changing Values
    Women and the Family in the Northern Colonies
    Ecological Transformation

The Plantation South
    The Tobacco Coast
    The Rice Coast
    The Backcountry
    Family Life in the South
    Enslaved Africans in the Southern Colonies
    Resistance and Rebellion
    Black Religion and Family

Contending for a Continent
    France's Inland Empire
    A Generation of War
    Spain's Frail North American Grip
    Cultural and Ecological Changes Among Interior Tribes

The Urban World of Commerce and Ideas
    Sinews of Trade
    The Artisan's World
    Urban Social Structure
    The Entrepreneurial Ethos
    The American Enlightenment

The Great Awakening
  Fading Faith
  The Awakeners' Message
  Revivalism in the Urban North
  Southern Revivalism
  Legacy of the Awakening

Political Life
  Structuring Colonial Governments
  The Crowd in Action
  The Growing Power of the Assemblies
  Local Politics
  The Spread of Whig Ideology

Conclusion: America in 1750

(2) SIGNIFICANT THEMES AND HIGHLIGHTS

1. In the first half of the eighteenth century, America was made up of several distinct regional societies, each in the process of growth and change. Beyond the Appalachians, extensive contact with France's growing inland empire and Spanish American settlements in the South and Southwest transformed Native American ways of life. English settlements, however, exploding in population, threatened Indian cultural cohesion the most. This chapter stresses the increasing complexity, adaption, and maturing of colonial English society. The eighteenth century provided opportunities for some, like William Phips; great gains for a few, like Boston merchant Andrew Belcher; but disappointment and privation for many others, like members of many Native American tribes.

2. The farming society of the North was characterized by widespread land ownership and a rough kind of economic equality. In the South, plantation society was marked by the emergence of a gentry class and a labor force almost entirely made up of black slaves, while the backcountry, still in the frontier stages and settled by thousands of Scots-Irish and German immigrants, lacked the sharp class distinctions of the tidewater region. Colonial cities, with their highly differentiated class structure and new commercial values, were on the "cutting edge" of change. In each area, women played an important but limited role in daily life.

3. Slavery became a primary source of labor and profits in the plantation south but was also closely bound up with economic life in the North. Slavery profoundly affected the lives of both white and black Americans and was an ironic comment on the notion of America as a place of refuge and hope.

4. The Great Awakening was more than a religious revival, for it produced patterns of thought and behavior that helped to fuel the Revolution. The course of the Great Awakening in Boston and Virginia vividly shows the way in which its message fused with local social and economic tensions to threaten established authority.

5. Although many historians focus on the changing political arrangements in the colonies in the first half of the eighteenth century as a means of preparing for a discussion of the Revolution, this chapter makes the point that the fluidity of American society itself must be understood as a prelude to the events of the 1770s.

(3) LEARNING GOALS

Familiarity with Basic Knowledge

After reading this chapter, you should be able to:

1. Name the major immigrant groups coming to the colonies in the early eighteenth century, describe their social backgrounds, find their destinations on the map, and summarize their relative opportunities for social and economic advancement.

2. Describe the cultural changes of the interior Indian tribes as a result of their contact with French, Spanish, and English settlements in economic, social, and domestic life; in their relation to the environment; in political organization; and in intertribal tensions.

3. Describe northern farm society and its most important social characteristics and problems, including family life and the ways in which the roles and rights of women changed in the colonies.

4. Give an account of the "profound social transition" of the Upper South, characterize the social and political nature of the southern gentry, and detail the social and economic differences between the tobacco and rice coasts and the backcountry.

5. Describe cultural features, such as religion and family, of enslaved African Americans during the seventeenth and eighteenth centuries.

6. Contrast the practice of slavery in the plantation south with the northern colonies.

7. Describe the urban social structure, including the merchant's pivotal role, and the work pattern and attitudes of urban artisans.

8. Explain the major events and message of the Great Awakening, including its comparative impact on New England and the southern colonies and its effects on colonial political life.

Practice in Historical Thinking Skills

After reading this chapter, you should be able to:

1. Compare and contrast the development and maturing of English society in the farming northern colonies, in the plantation South, and in colonial cities.

2. Discuss the foundations of colonial political structures and ideology, including what colonists meant by a political balance of power and how it matched the reality of Whig ideology and local political arrangements.

3. Analyze how the changing mixture of ethnic, racial, religious, and regional settlements in North America, as well as class differences, provided awkward incongruities and threats of social unrest in the various societies of the New World.

(4) IMPORTANT DATES AND NAMES TO KNOW

1662	Half-Way Covenant in New England
1682	La Salle canoes down Mississippi River and claims Louisiana for France
1689-1697	King William's War
1700	Spanish establish first mission in Arizona
1701-1713	Queen Anne's War
1704	*Boston News-Letter,* first regular colonial newspaper, published
1712	First northern slave revolt erupts in New York City
1713	Peace of Utrecht
1714	Beginning of Scots-Irish and German Immigration
1715-1730	Volume of slave trade doubles
1718	French settle New Orleans
1720s	Natural increase of African population begins
1732	Benjamin Franklin publishes first *Poor Richard's Almanack*
1734-1736	Great Awakening begins in Northampton, Massachusetts

1735	Zenger acquitted of seditious libel in New York
1739	Slave revolt in Stono, South Carolina
1739-1740	Whitefield's first American tour spreads Great Awakening
1740s	Slaves compose 90 percent of population on Carolina rice coast Indigo becomes staple crop in Lower South
1747	Impressment Riot in Boston
1750s	Quakers initiate campaign to halt slave trade and end slavery
1760	Africans compose 20 percent of colonial population
1760s-1770s	Spanish establish California mission system
1769	American Philosophical Society founded at Philadelphia

Other Names to Know

Jonathan Edwards	Benjamin Lay
John Bartram	James Davenport
Andrew Belcher	Cotton Mather

(5) GLOSSARY OF IMPORTANT TERMS

artisan: a skilled worker, using hand tools, usually in a small shop, such as a carpenter, cooper, shoemaker, or silversmith

franchise: the right to vote, widespread among colonial free white males

Half-Way Covenant: an attempt by New England clergy in 1662 to counteract declining church membership by allowing the children of church members to join the church even though they had not experienced salvation; they were, however, denied voting and communion rights

power of the purse: the power of colonial legislatures in the eighteenth century to initiate money bills, specifying the amount to be raised and its uses

(6) ENRICHMENT IDEAS

1. Examine the contents of your household. What do the items of your house reflect about your culture and values? What do they reveal about the society you live in? What do you need to survive? What items would be considered luxury items? Referring to "Recovering the Past," compare and contrast the possession of the Chandler brothers with Robert Oliver's. What might the possessions reveal about class tensions during the eighteenth century?

2. If you live in the East, you will probably be able to visit a historic house that dates from this period. In the South, see the country houses of the new gentry class or their town houses in Williamsburg. In the North and the Mid-Atlantic states, there are fine old houses of the merchant class and often of German immigrants. What do the houses suggest about daily life and about the class structure of the eighteenth century? Do you see evidences of slaves or servants? What suggestions are there about the lives of women and children? What would you conclude about the nature of work and leisure? Does the historic preservation of a house present a romanticized version of life in the past?

3. Consider recent episodes of religious revivalism. What has changed and what is the same?

4. Does the existence of pluralistic ethnic, racial, religious, and regional groups strengthen or threaten American cultural and political life today?

(7) SAMPLE TEST AND EXAMINATION QUESTIONS

Multiple choice: Choose the best answer.

1. Most German and Scots-Irish immigrants settled
    a. in the nation's interior.
    b. along the Atlantic coast.
    c. only in the South.
    d. in major cities.

2. The fastest-growing area in the early eighteenth century was
    a. New England.
    b. South Carolina.
    c. the northern frontier.
    d. the area south of Pennsylvania.

3. Most eighteenth-century emigrants were
    a. wealthy landed aristocrats.
    b. middle-class artisans and yeoman farmers.
    c. slaves and indentured servants.
    d. prisoners.

4. Most eighteenth-century indentured servants
   a. lived long prosperous lives in North America.
   b. were brought from Africa.
   c. usually were able to buy land after serving their time.
   d. found the system harsh and even deadly in some cases.

5. Slavery in the northern colonies during the eighteenth century
   a. was prohibited by law.
   b. was more repressive than in the southern colonies.
   c. was similar to southern plantation slavery
   d. utilized slaves as primarily artisans, farmhands, and personal servants.

6. Compared to slaves in the West Indies and Brazil, slaves in North America
   a. started many more massive slave insurrections.
   b. had little opportunity to develop a culture because of their short life span.
   c. lived in a relatively healthy environment.
   d. has a less balanced gender ratio.

7. Slave resistance in North America did not usually take the form of
   a. avoiding work.
   b. running away.
   c. overt rebellion.
   d. arson and breaking work equipment.

8. Barriers to slave family life during the eighteenth century included
   a. the abrupt sale of husband, wife, or child to another owner.
   b. white male exploitation of enslaved Black women.
   c. both (a) and (b).
   d. neither (a) nor (b).

9. In the backcountry of the South, settlers
   a. were primarily German and Scots-Irish.
   b. lived in a subsistence society of small farms.
   c. had few institutions.
   d. all of the above.

10. In the eighteenth century, what percentage of Americans lived in cities?
    a. 5 percent.
    b. 10 percent.
    c. 15 percent.
    d. 20 percent.

11. Urban artisans
    a. expected a rapid rise to ownership of their own shops.
    b. took fierce pride in their craft, role as community leaders, and independence.
    c. viewed themselves as "mere mechanicks."
    d. did better economically in New England than Philadelphia.

12. All of the following statements about eighteenth-century cities are true EXCEPT that they
    a. showed an increasing gap between rich and poor.
    b. showed evidence of a new entrepreneurial ethic.
    c. were marked by frequent episodes of intensely violent social conflict.
    d. devised new ways of dealing with the poor.

13. In the early eighteenth century, most Americans
    a. were Congregationalists.
    b. were Anglicans.
    c. were Baptists.
    d. belonged to no church at all.

14. The Great Awakening
    a. decreased the number of religious denominations.
    b. undermined church-state ties.
    c. undermined community diversity.
    d. encouraged higher education by emphasizing that the clergy should be educated within the established church.

15. American political assumptions included the belief that
    a. only free men with property should vote.
    b. only men of wealth and social status should hold positions of political power.
    c. people had the right to protest openly if power was abused.
    d. all of the above.

16. In the mid-eighteenth century, colonial assemblies
    a. gradually gained more powers, such as that of initiating money bills.
    b. were mainly advisory bodies.
    c. were regularly dissolved by royal governors.
    d. ignored instructions from local constituencies.

Essays

1. The three items under "Practice in Historical Thinking Skills" can serve as the basis for essays.

2. The Great Awakening transformed American life and thought in significant ways. Support this statement using appropriate evidence.

3. Rising tensions among social classes characterized colonial society in the eighteenth century and made political and religious struggles bitter. Discuss with evidence.

4. Explain how religion and family could be used a means of survival for the slaves and a means of social control for the slave owners.

Identify and Interpret: Quotation
(that is, state who, what, where, when, and why significant)

The bow of God's wrath is bent, and the arrow made ready on the string; and justice bends the arrow at your heart, and strains the bow; and it is nothing but the mere pleasure of God, and that of an angry God, without any promise or obligation at all, that keeps the arrow one moment from being made drunk with your blood. Thus are all you that never passed under a great change of heart, by the mighty power of the Spirit of God upon your souls; all you that were never born again, and made new creatures. . . . The God that holds you over the pit of hell, much as one holds a spider or some loathsome insect over the fire, abhors you, and is dreadfully provoked; his wrath towards you burns like fire; he looks upon you as worthy of nothing else, but to be cast into the fire.

5

The Strains of Empire

(1) CHAPTER OUTLINE

Shoemaker Ebenezer MacIntosh finds that the Stamp Act crisis offers him opportunities for influence and prominence. He leads mobs during the Stamp Act crisis protesting against both English authority and Boston's elite.

The Climactic Seven Years' War
- War and the Management of Empire
- Outbreak of Hostilities
- Tribal Strategies
- Consequences of the Seven Years' War

The Crisis with England
- Sugar, Currency, and Stamps
- Stamp Act Riots
- Gathering Storm Clouds
- The Growing Rift

The Ideology of Revolutionary Republicanism
- A Plot Against Liberty
- Revitalizing American Society

The Turmoil of a Rebellious People
- Urban People
- Patriot Women
- Protesting Farmers

Conclusion: On the Brink of Revolution

(2) SIGNIFICANT THEMES AND HIGHLIGHTS

1. Beginning with Ebenezer MacIntosh, the chapter stresses the role of common people in the events leading to the American Revolution rather than placing the usual emphasis on famous founding fathers.

2. The chapter shows that there was widespread group support for not one but two American revolutions. As MacIntosh's activities suggest, the "dual American Revolution" combined an external struggle to sever colonial ties to England with an internal struggle for control and reform of colonial society. The colonists sought liberation from English rule. But they also sought to combat the aristocratic, elitist nature of colonial society. The first revolution, marked by violent conflict with England, was the War for American Independence; the second, which involved intense class resentments, is called the American Revolution. The first ended in the Declaration of Independence; the second continued long into the next century.

3. The chapter not only explains these two revolutions but also interweaves colonial history with events in Europe and with the Native American tribes of the interior forests. The perspectives, survival strategies, and cultural changes of the Iroquois, Creek, and Cherokee are seen to be just as important as those of the British, French, and American colonists. The harmful effects of the Seven Years' War loom large in this chapter, especially on groups like the urban laboring poor, backcountry farmers, and women.

4. These groups each had their own struggles against concentrated wealth and power. But these differences were fruitful, for with educated lawyers and rich merchants and planters they fashioned a political ideology of revolutionary republicanism.

(3) LEARNING GOALS

Familiarity with Basic Knowledge

After reading this chapter, you should be able to:

1. Make a clear statement distinguishing between the War for American Independence and the American Revolution.

2. Describe the issues at stake in the series of wars of empire between England, Spain, France, and the several Native American Indian tribes, and outline the major developments and consequences of the Seven Years' War.

3. Outline the steps in the crisis with England between 1763 and 1776 leading to the War for American Independence.

4. Explain the essential issues and elements involved in the ideology of revolutionary republicanism.

5. Describe the grievances and concerns of ordinary Americans between 1763 and 1776, explaining how urban people, women, and farmers understood their "liberties" and "natural rights" in the early 1770s.

Practice in Historical Thinking Skills

After reading this chapter, you should be able to:

1. Discuss the two revolutions going on in the British colonies between 1763 and 1776, explaining the main characteristics of each and indicating which revolution you think motivated the American people more in the 1760s and 1770s.

2. Assess the mutual impact and influence of the interior Indian tribes, the American colonists, and the British and French on one another in the mid-eighteenth century.

3. Identify the chapter author's interpretation of "the nature of the American Revolution" and cite the evidence presented to support that point of view.

(4) IMPORTANT DATES AND NAMES TO KNOW

1696	Parliament establishes Board of Trade
1701	Iroquois set policy of neutrality
1702-1713	Queen Anne's War
1713	Peace of Utrecht
1733	Molasses Act
1739-1742	War of Jenkins' Ear
1744-1748	King George's War
1754	Albany conference
1755	Braddock defeated by French and Indian allies Acadians expelled from Nova Scotia
1756-1763	Seven Years' War
1759	Wolfe defeats the French at Quebec
1759-1761	Cherokee War against the English
1760s	Economic slump
1763	Treaty of Paris ends Seven Years' War Proclamation Line limits westward expansion

1764	Sugar and Currency acts
	Pontiac's Rebellion in Ohio valley
1765	Colonists resist Stamp Act
	Virginia House of Burgess issues Stamp Act resolutions
1766	Declaratory Act
	Tenant rent war in New York
	Slave insurrections in South Carolina
1767	Townshend duties imposed
1768	British troops occupy Boston
1770	"Boston Massacre"
	Townshend duties repealed (except on tea)
1771	North Carolina Regulators defeated
1772	*Gaspee* incident in Rhode Island
1773	Tea Act provokes Boston Tea Party
1774	"Intolerable Acts"
	First Continental Congress meets in Philadelphia

Other Names to Know

General James Wolfe	Pontiac	Governor Thomas Hutchinson
William Pitt	George Grenville	General Thomas Gage
Patrick Henry	Lord North	Phillis Wheatley
John Adams	Samuel Adams	Andrew Oliver

(5) GLOSSARY OF IMPORTANT TERMS

nonimportation and nonconsumption agreements: economic boycotts, as individual colonists pledged neither to import nor to use any British articles but rather to go without or to make their own, the main tactic of colonists protesting the Townshend duties and the Tea Act

privateers: privately outfitted ships licensed by colonial governments to attack French merchant shipping during the Seven Years' War

revolutionary republicanism: A set of political ideals developed in the American Revolutionary era that emphasized anti-monarchy, liberty in balance with power, and political equality in tension with rule by an aristocracy of talent

(6) ENRICHMENT IDEAS

1. Study the "Recovering the Past" section for this chapter, noting how the poetry of Phillis Wheatley during the Revolutionary War era contributes to your understanding of the American resistance to British policies. Evaluate Wheatley's comparison between the plight of the colonist to that of African slaves, indirectly challenging the institution of slavery in the United States. How effective is poetry in mobilizing political energy?

2. If you live in a rural area or small town (especially in the Midwest), it is likely that your local newspaper will advertise several auctions of the property and household belongings of family farms in the process of dissolution. Go to an auction or two, and note how the items for sale reflect social class.

3. If you live in the East, you can visit such Revolutionary sites as Philadelphia, Boston, and Lexington and Concord, as well as battle sites at Bunker Hill (Breed's Hill), Saratoga, Trenton, Valley Forge, Brandywine, and Yorktown. What interpretation is provided at these sites? Which "American Revolution" is presented? Is there any indication of the social tensions of the inner war? How do you explain the approach taken at these Revolutionary-era sites?

(7) SAMPLE TEST AND EXAMINATION QUESTIONS

Multiple choice: Choose the best answer.

1. In seeking to survive the wars of empire in North America, the Native American Indian tribes
   a. depended on French friendship.
   b. formed treaty alliances with the more numerous British.
   c. sought to play European powers against each other.
   d. formed intertribal confederacies.

2. Most at stake for the European powers in the wars of empire was
   a. the economic and political value of North American land and resources.
   b. religious freedom.
   c. national pride.
   d. treaty obligations to the Indians.

3. The Seven Years' War
   a. spurred colonial prosperity.
   b. required heavy taxes.
   c. rendered the colonies vulnerable to fluctuations in the British economy.
   d. all of the above.

4. The British finally turned the tide of battle to their side in the Seven Years' War when they
   a. pursued William Pitt's policies in North America.
   b. defeated the Iroquois allies of the French.
   c. convinced the American colonists to share more of the fighting burdens of the war.
   d. dispatched General Braddock to attack French forts.

5. After the Treaty of Paris, economic prosperity in the colonies
   a. surged because of captured French resources.
   b. turned to depression, especially among the laboring classes in coastal towns.
   c. remained high because of war profiteering.
   d. was largely unchanged.

6. The Stamp Act riots
   a. happened only in Boston.
   b. revealed how united all American classes were in opposing British authority.
   c. politicized the American people against both English rule and internal elites.
   d. convinced Parliament to limit its authority over the colonies.

7. The Sugar Act
   a. doubled duties on sugar imported from the West Indies.
   b. kept duties the same but improved enforcement.
   c. cut duties in half but improved enforcement through strengthening the vice-admiralty courts.
   d. required stamps on every gallon of imported molasses.

8. In June 1772, a British proposal that deeply threatened and angered colonists in Massachusetts was one
   a. to tax window glass.
   b. to have the British government rather than colonial assemblies pay the salaries of royal governors.
   c. to limit town meetings to once a month.
   d. to close the port of Boston permanently.

9. Which is in the correct chronological order?
   a. Tea Act, Tea Party, Continental Congress, Intolerable Acts.
   b. Tea Act, Intolerable Acts, Tea Party, Continental Congress.
   c. Tea Act, Tea Party, Intolerable Acts, Continental Congress.
   d. Intolerable Acts, Continental Congress, Tea Act, Tea Party.

10. In the face of tougher expressions of British authority, by the end of 1774 the colonists had
    a. knuckled under to British rule.
    b. created armed militia units to harass British troops and bully local Loyalist merchants.
    c. sought aid from the French.
    d. begun electing their own provincial assemblies to draft declarations of independence.

11. The ideology of revolutionary republicanism included all of the following EXCEPT
    a. a call for the guaranteeing of English liberties.
    b. a demand for the end to corruption in government.
    c. independence through a guarantee of property rights.
    d. pure leveling of society through economic equality.

12. Revolutionary agitation for equality and rights among social groups was expressed by all of the following EXCEPT
    a. urban artisans.
    b. backcountry farmers.
    c. Most Virginia planters.
    d. women.

13. The dual American Revolution
    a. united all colonial classes in a common effort.
    b. exposed class tensions in the process of struggling against British tyranny.
    c. tore the colonies apart.
    d. put the colonists at war with both the French and British.

14. The North Carolina Regulators
    a. were an example of urban insurrection.
    b. won their demands without bloodshed.
    c. were comprised mainly of farmers from the eastern part of the state.
    d. demonstrated lower-class resentment of corrupt authority

15. Colonists disliked the Quebec Act of 1774 because it
    a. cut off western lands from speculators and recognized the rights of Catholics.
    b. put New England under the political control of Quebec.
    c. was passed without the consent of Parliament.
    d. gave away land to various Indian tribes.

Identify and show a relationship between each of the following pairs:

Pontiac	*and*	Proclamation Line of 1763
"Liberty Tree"	*and*	Andrew Oliver
Thomas Hutchinson	*and*	Samuel Adams
William Pitt	*and*	Fort Duquesne
James Wolfe	*and*	Thomas Gage
George Grenville	*and*	Patrick Henry
John Hancock	*and*	Ebenezer MacIntosh
Sons of Liberty	*and*	Philadelphia militia
Stamp Act	*and*	Townshend Acts

Essays

1. Items 1–3 under "Practice in Historical Thinking Skills" in the "Learning Goals" section can be used as practice essay questions.

2. To ignore the role of Native Americans in the pre-Revolutionary era is to ignore a very real factor in the coming struggle. Discuss with suitable evidence.

3. Even with better will and more compromises on both sides, it would have been difficult to prevent the American War for Independence. It was, in short, inevitable. The "American Revolution," however, was not. Discuss.

4. It has been said that "the American Revolution was not made but prevented." Discuss what you think this means and the extent to which you agree.

Map Question:

Locate the following on the accompanying map.

1. Lake Champlain
2. Iroquois Confederacy
3. Cherokee nation
4. Ohio River valley
5. Fort Duquesne
6. New York City
7. Philadelphia

8. Charleston, South Carolina
9. Fort Ticonderoga
10. Creek nation
11. Jamestown
12. Fort Niagara
13. Boston
14. Quebec City

PART TWO (Chapters 6–9)

A REVOLUTIONARY PEOPLE 1775–1828

The American Revolution not only marked an epic military victory over the powerful mother country, but set the course of national development in ways that still affect American society. Members of the Revolutionary generation were inspired by the idea that once they were free from England, they would build a model society based on principles of freedom and equality. Even as the battle for independence raged, they embarked on the task of building new forms of government and transforming their social, religious, and economic lives. This attempt to construct a *novus ordo seclorum,* a new order of the ages, continued beyond the Revolutionary era and continues yet today.

Chapter 6, "A People in Revolution," traces the impact of the Revolutionary call to arms on the various groups—male and female, white, black, and Native American—that made up American society and traces the exhilarating yet divisive efforts to fashion a new, republican political order. Chapter 7, "Consolidating the Revolution," examines the critical years of the 1780s, when the new nation struggled to forge national unity following the Revolutionary War and to find security in a hostile Atlantic world. Out of that struggle and the continuing competition for political power in the states emerged a great debate over the country's governmental structure. That debate led to the replacement of the Articles of Confederation with a new constitution, which in turn helped to create a stronger government. Learning to live under the new constitution during the 1790s is the focus for Chapter 8, "Creating a Nation." During those tumultuous years, charged with the reverberations of the French Revolution and fierce disagreements about the government's role in economic affairs, Federalists and Jeffersonians battled for control of the new government and the chance to shape the nation's future.

Chapter 9, "Society and Politics in the Early Republic," delves into the political and diplomatic developments of the first three decades of the nineteenth century, when the young nation expanded rapidly beyond the Appalachians, acquired vast new territories, fought a series of wars with Indian nations and a second war against England, and moved toward a new party system, all under the presidencies of three Virginia Democratic-Republicans—Jefferson, Madison, and Monroe—and one New Englander, John Quincy Adams. This chapter examines the impact of the Haitian Revolution and the Latin American independence movements on American foreign policy. Chapter 9 also investigates efforts by the American people in the areas of education, women's rights, and slavery to perfect their republican society in keeping with the lofty principles of the Revolution.

6

A People in Revolution

(1) CHAPTER OUTLINE

"Long Bill" Scott, wounded and captured by the British, explains that the ambition to better himself rather than patriotism led him to join the Revolutionary army. Still, in the next few years, he escapes twice from the British, fights in New York and Rhode Island, and volunteers for the navy. The main effect of the war for Long Bill and his family, however, was not military exploits but poverty, sickness, and death.

Bursting the Colonial Bonds
  The Final Rupture
  Thomas Paine's *Common Sense*
  Declaring Independence

The War for American Independence
  The War in the North
  Congress and the Articles of Confederation
  The War Moves South
  Native Americans in the Revolution
  The Devastation of the Iroquois
  Negotiating Peace
  The Ingredients of Victory

The Experience of War
  Recruiting an Army
  The Casualties of Combat
  Civilians and the War
  The Loyalists
  African Americans and the War

The Ferment of Revolutionary Politics
  Mobilizing the People
  A Republican Ideology
  Forming New Governments
  Different Paths to the Republican Goal
  Women and the Limits of Republican Citizenship

Conclusion: The Crucible of Revolution

(2) SIGNIFICANT THEMES AND HIGHLIGHTS

1. As Long Bill Scott's sad but heroic story reveals, people in America during the Revolution struggled not only to create a nation but even more to improve their own lives. This chapter emphasizes the private struggles and hardships and the disrupted lives of people in America during the Revolutionary War rather than the battles and public policy decisions of the war. The chapter continues the account of class divisions in American society during wartime, which underlines the theme of a "dual revolution."

2. This chapter creates a mood that underlines the startling facts that the American Revolutionary War was the longest war in American history (except one), the most costly in per capita casualties (except one), and (without exception) the most damaging in terms of per capita victimization of civilians and the disruption and disarray of economic life.

3. It was in state politics that Americans transformed and expressed the political meaning of the Revolution. The making of new state governments involved converting the ideology of revolutionary republicanism into action, first by writing state constitutions and second by resolving the thorny issues of Revolutionary times.

4. Although many more ordinary people—white farmers, small shopkeepers, urban artisans, and the like—were politicized and joined the political process, there were limits to republican representation and political participation. Large numbers of Americans—women, blacks, Indians—were excluded from the new political system.

(3) LEARNING GOALS

Familiarity with Basic Knowledge

After reading this chapter, you should be able to:

1. Describe the major British and American strategies in the American Revolution and state how well they worked.

2. Explain five reasons why the Americans defeated the British and won the war.

3. Describe the economic costs of the war to commerce, agriculture, and manufacturing.

4. Explain how the war affected slaves, Loyalists, and Native American Indians, especially the Iroquois.

5. List the questions that the early republican politicians (or anyone, for that matter) asked when thinking about creating new governments.

6. State a few key differences between the Pennsylvania and Massachusetts state constitutions.

7. State ways in which Americans were politicized during the Revlutionary era.

8. Describe American sentiment on women's political participation during the post war era.

Practice in Historical Thinking Skills

After reading this chapter, you should be able to:

1. Analyze how the American people made the shift from separating from an imperial system to the creation of a republican form of government.

2. Assess the extent to which the American Revolution, on balance, was good or bad for slaves, northern farmers, Loyalists, Native Americans, wealthy Patriots, and ordinary citizens.

(4) IMPORTANT DATES AND NAMES TO KNOW

1775	Lexington and Concord
	Second Continental Congress
	Lord Dunmore's proclamation to slaves and servants in Virginia
	Iroquois Six Nations pledge neutrality
1776	Thomas Paine's *Common Sense*
	British evacuate Boston and seize New York City
	Declaration of Independence
	Eight states draft constitutions
	Cherokee raids and American retaliations
1777	British occupy Philadelphia
	Most Iroquois join the British
	American win victory at Saratoga
	Washington's army winters at Valley Forge
1778	War shifts to the South
	Savannah falls to the British
	French treaty of alliance and commerce
1779	Massachusetts state constitutional convention
	Sullivan destroys Iroquois villages in New York
1780	Massachusetts constitution ratified
	Charleston surrenders to the British

1780s	Destruction of Iroquois Confederacy
1781	Cornwallis surrenders at Yorktown
	Articles of Confederation ratified by states
1783	Peace treaty with England signed in Paris
	Massachusetts Supreme Court abolishes slavery
	King's Commission on American Loyalists begins work

Other Names to Know

Joesph Brant	Thomas Danforth	John Adams
General William Howe	Robert Morris	Abigail Adams
Charles Grannier de Vergennes	Thomas Peters	Esther DeBerdt Reed
John Dickinson	King George III	Nathaneal Greene

(5) GLOSSARY OF IMPORTANT TERMS

bills of credit: paper money issued by the continental government and backed by government credit to finance the war

Loyalists: Americans loyal to the crown during the Revolution who actively supported, sympathized with, or fought on the British side

partisan warfare: American strategy (called guerrilla warfare today) under Nathanael Greene in the South whereby several small, highly mobile bands of soldiers waged hit-and-run attacks on British troops rather than standing together as one army

privateering: government chartering of private vessels to prey upon English merchant ships

sovereignty: source or locus of ultimate power; for republican ideology, sovereignty resided in the people

(6) ENRICHMENT IDEAS

1. After examining the military muster rolls in the "Recovering the Past" section for this chapter, discuss the social composition of the revolutionary army. How did it change over time? What types of people took arms for the Revolution? How would social historians use military rolls to describe and analyze more recent wars?

2. If you live in the East, visit Revolutionary War battle sites at Boston, New York, Trenton, Princeton, Bennington, Saratoga, Brandywine, Savannah, Charleston, Cowpens, Guilford Court House, or Yorktown. Imagine yourself a common soldier at one of those battles. Write a letter home or a diary entry describing what it was like.

3. Imagine you are a former crown official—or a slave—or a New England farmer—or a northern artisan—or a Virginia Patriot slave owner—or a woman living on the frontier—or some other colonist. What reasons would you give to explain your position for or against the war?

4. Difficult material like political ideology is sometimes easier to understand by representing abstract ideas in some sort of visual way. Construct a chart on revolutionary republican ideology, showing such things as political focus and structures (branches and levels of government), ways of balancing liberty and power, and ideas about equality and who should rule; for example, a continuum:

LIBERTY	POWER/ORDER
HAPPINESS	PROPERTY

the P E O P L E

or a diagram showing John Adams's "Thoughts on Government" and his proposal for the Massachusetts state constitution:

LEGISLATIVE		EXECUTIVE	JUDICIARY
REPRESENTATIVE	*SENATE*		*GOVERNOR*
ASSEMBLY	(Council)	(President)	
·democratic	·aristocratic	·independent	·separate
·the many	·the few	·the one	and distinct
·liberty	·property	·balancer	

(7) SAMPLE TEST AND EXAMINATION QUESTIONS

Multiple choice: Choose the best answer.

1. The primary strategy of the American continental forces against the British was
    a. defensive, surviving by avoiding major battles.
    b. aggressive, seeking to split British forces in half.
    c. to hide while waiting for French help.
    d. to let the British have coastal cities while protecting the frontier against Indians.

2. His pamphlet, *Common Sense*, encouraged America's revolt:
   a. Samuel Adams.
   b. Thomas Paine.
   c. Patrick Henry.
   d. John Hancock.

3. The Americans were successful at the Paris treaty convention because
   a. they had the support of the French foreign minister, Vergennes.
   b. they ignored the French and negotiated directly with the British.
   c. they held Cornwallis hostage until they received generous terms.
   d. Franklin and Adams respected instructions from Congress.

4. As the war dragged on, the continental army was made up largely of
   a. poor men conscripted or hired as substitutes by wealthy men in towns filling their quotas.
   b. city merchants.
   c. a polyglot mixture of local militias.
   d. eager volunteer enlisted men.

5. The Declaration of Independence
   a. was accepted exactly as Jefferson's committee had written it.
   b. was ratified after all thirteen delegations voted "yes."
   c. was based on earlier justification of American resistance previously stated theories of government.
   d. was jeered by most Philadelphians when it was first read to them.

6. The American Patriots won the war against Great Britain for all of following reasons EXCEPT
   a. the administrative talents and determination of General Washington.
   b. British caution and lack of will.
   c. the enormous drain on England's financial resources.
   d. the military skill of the state militias.

7. The battle of Saratoga
   a. was a critical defeat for the colonial army.
   b. saw the colonists defeat an army of German mercenaries.
   c. prompted France to join the colonial struggle against England.
   d. was won by the colonists because of General Washington's brilliant strategy.

8. Women contributed to the War for Independence by in all the following ways EXCEPT
   a. joining the army at the same rate as men.
   b. raising money.
   c. publishing pamphlets on revolutionary politics.
   d. spinning and weaving clothing formerly made by the British.

9. The Iroquois resolve to remain neutral during the Revolution
   a. reflected a new strategy of surviving conflicts among whites in the New World.
   b. was abandoned in 1777 when most of the Iroquois nations followed the advice of Joseph Brant and joined the British against the Americans.
   c. resulted in generous land concessions under the Treaty of Paris.
   d. was abandoned to side with the French in exchange for trade goods, arms, and protection.

10. All of the following were included in the Treaty of Paris (1783) EXCEPT
    a. the western boundary of the United States was set at the Mississippi River.
    b. all debts between citizens of the two countries were invalidated.
    c. the British recognized the independence of the United States of America.
    d. the Americans promised to restore Loyalists' rights and properties.

11. The Pennsylvania constitution provided for
    a. an executive governor without veto power.
    b. two representative legislatures.
    c. an executive created out of the assembly.
    d. no governor.

12. The Massachusetts constitution was based on John Adams's ideas of
    a. the predominance of aristocratic power.
    b. a weak executive branch.
    c. mixed and balanced separate branches of government.
    d. power in the lower house.

13. The American people were politicized during the American Revolution by
    a. ministers.
    b. an outpouring of political pamphlets and newspapers.
    c. the frequency of state-level elections.
    d. all of the above.

14. For the colonial soldiers in the Revolution, which proved most deadly?
    a. Indian attacks.
    b. British bullets.
    c. Diseases and sickness.
    d. French cannons.

Date and put the following events in the correct chronological order:
(This includes material from chapters 5 and 6: the entire revolutionary era.)

Lexington and Concord	Boston Tea Party
Treaty of Paris	Stamp Act
French treaty of alliance and commerce	Battle of Saratoga
End of Seven Years' War	Declaration of Independence
Yorktown	"Boston Massacre"

Identify and show a relationship between each of the following pairs:

Joseph Brant	*and*	Loyalists
Yorktown	*and*	Treaty of Paris
partisan warfare	*and*	Valley Forge
Saratoga	*and*	French treaty of alliance and commerce
John Adams	*and*	Abigail Adams

Essays

1. Assess the extent to which the American Revolution, on balance, was good or bad for *five* of the following groups: northern farmers, Virginia slave owners, enslaved Africans, free African Americans, Native Americans, Loyalists, urban artisans and shopkeepers, frontier women.

2. Assess how well Americans were able to fulfill their revolutionary republican ideology in the war and the postwar era.

3. Show how the ideology of republicanism, which developed during the war, reflected the colonial experience with England prior to the war.

4. Why did the American colonists win the War for Independence?

Identify and Interpret: Quotation
(that is, state who, what, where, when, and why significant)

I cannot say that I think you are very generous to the ladies; for, whilst you are proclaiming peace and goodwill to men, emancipating all nations, you insist upon retaining an absolute power over wives. But you must remember, that arbitrary power is like most other things which are very hard, very liable to be broken; and, notwithstanding all your wise laws and maxims, we have it in our power, not only to free ourselves, but to subdue our masters, and, without violence, throw both your natural and legal authority at our feet.

7

Consolidating the Revolution

(1) CHAPTER OUTLINE

Timothy Bloodworth of New Hanover County, North Carolina, rises from humble origins and gains a substantial position in his community and the respect of his neighbors. Although he becomes a delegate to the Confederation Congress in 1784, he soon loses confidence in the Articles of Confederationand supports the call for a special convention to meet in Philadelphia in 1787. When he views the constitution that emerges from that convention, however, he fears that the gains of the Revolution will be lost. He works tirelessly to defeat the new proposal. As a result of his efforts and the efforts of men like him, North Carolina only endorsed the new union when the Congress had forwarded a national bill of rights to the state for its approval.

Struggling with the Peacetime Agenda
    Demobilizing the Army
    Opening the West
    Wrestling with the National Debt
    Surviving in a Hostile Atlantic World

Sources of Political Conflict
    Separating Church and State
    Slavery Under Attack
    Politics and the Economy

Political Tumult in the States
    The Limits of Republican Experimentation
    Shays's Rebellion

Toward a New National Government
    The Rise of Federalism
    The Grand Convention
    Drafting the Constitution
    Federalists Versus Anti-Federalists
    The Struggle over Ratification
    The Social Geography of Ratification

Conclusion: Completing the Revolution

(2) SIGNIFICANT THEMES AND HIGHLIGHTS

1. As the anecdote of Timothy Bloodworth suggests, this chapter explores the uncertain world facing Americans after the Revolutionary War had ended. Many feared the new government would not be able to assure settlement of the country's interior or pay off the massive war debt. The new nation was a weak newcomer in a world still dominated by powers like Great Britain.

2. The frantic pace of political experimentation on the state level moderated after 1783 as conservative arrangements replaced some of the radical ones passed only a few years earlier. As Shays's Rebellion suggested, however, many had not forgotten the cries for equal rights and popular consent that had been so powerfully expressed in 1776.

3. This chapter presents the political controversies marking the writing and ratification of the Constitution and explains the struggle for ratification of that document.

(3) LEARNING GOALS

Familiarity with Basic Knowledge

After reading this chapter, you should be able to:

1. Describe the terms of the land ordinances of 1785 and 1787 and the ideas behind the conquest strategy.

2. Discuss problems with the American economy after the war.

3. Explain the causes and consequences of Shays's Rebellion.

4. Describe the movement for full religious liberty.

5. Describe the reasons for dissatisfaction with the Articles of Confederation.

6. State the major compromises worked out at the Constitutional Convention and the major features of the original Constitution—its organizational format and the most significant allocations of power, rights, and responsibilities.

7. Outline the major arguments of Federalists and Anti-Federalists in the debates over ratification of the Constitution.

Practice in Historical Thinking Skills

After reading this chapter, you should be able to:

1. Assess how well Americans were able to fulfill their revolutionary republican ideology in the post war era.

2. Discuss the impact of Thomas Jefferson's "Bill for Establishing Religious Freedom."

3. Compare and contrast the different ideological positions regarding slavery.

4. Explain the reasons for the success of the Federalists in writing and securing the ratification of the Constitution.

5. Analyze how the Constitution changed and strengthened the government that had existed under the Articles of Confederation.

6. Describe the different political and social perspectives of the Federalists and Anti-Federalists.

(4) IMPORTANT DATES AND NAMES TO KNOW

1780s	Pennsylvania begins gradual abolition of slavery Virginia and Maryland debate abolition of slavery
1784	Treaty of Fort Stanwix with the Iroquois Spain closes the Mississippi River to American navigation
1785	Treaty of Hopewell with the Cherokee Land Ordinance for the Northwest Territory Jay-Gardoqui negotiations
1786	Virginia adopts Bill for Establishing Religious Freedom Annapolis Convention calls for revision of Articles of Confederation
1786-1787	Shays's Rebellion
1787	Northwest Ordinance Constitutional Convention *Federalist Papers* published by Hamilton, Jay, and Madison
1788	Constitution ratified

Other Names to Know

William Paterson	Luther Martin
John Trumbull	Robert Morris

(5) GLOSSARY OF IMPORTANT TERMS

federalism: a system where political power is divided between a central (national) government and smaller governmental units called states or provinces

ordinance: a governmental law or regulation

ratification: formal sanctioning of a document such as a proposed constitution or treaty

relief ("stay") laws: state laws desired by debtors and farmers in hard times that would suspend the collection of private debts and the foreclosure of farms for a specified period

(6) ENRICHMENT IDEAS

1. Find an Indian treaty for the Native Americans in your region and discover what it suggests about the attitudes and values of both the white and Native American treaty-makers.

2. The complete text of the United States Constitution is found in the Appendix of *The American People*. Read and study the Constitution, breaking it down into its major parts, and identify the five or so most significant points to remember in each part.

3. Make a chart contrasting the major differences between the Declaration of Independence and the Constitution over their primary purposes, the quality and style of language, political ideology, assumptions about human nature and ends of government, and how to achieve political change.

(7) SAMPLE TEST AND EXAMINATION QUESTIONS

Multiple choice: Choose the best answer.

1. After the Revolution, the Confederation Congress
    a. successfully opened western lands.
    b. quelled Indian resistance to white western migration.
    c. was unable to open the interior.
    d. gave all western lands to speculators.

2. Shays's Rebellion revealed that
   a. farmers wanted more gold coins in circulation.
   b. authority under the Articles of Confederation was too weak.
   c. the American Revolution had succeeded in shifting the balance of power from the rich to the poor.
   d. the court system was responsive to the needs of the people.

3. The Federalists believed all of the following EXCEPT that
   a. the national government should be stronger.
   b. there were "natural distinctions" between people.
   c. there was a crisis threatening the nation's survival.
   d. the states should assume more powers.

4. After the Revolution, the Confederation Congress treated Native Americans of the interior
   a. as if they were sovereign nations.
   b. as if they were military foes.
   c. no differently than they had in colonial times.
   d. as if they were conquered peoples.

5. The Virginia Plan differed most significantly from the New Jersey Plan by calling for
   a. a bicameral Congress and a whole new national government.
   b. revision of the Articles of Confederation by letting Congress choose a president.
   c. revision of the Articles by providing for equal representation in both houses of Congress.
   d. the abolition of the executive branch.

6. The Constitution clearly shows that the founding fathers
   a. wanted to abolish slavery.
   b. were prepared to lay the groundwork for eventual equal rights between whites and blacks.
   c. provided for the protection of the institution of slavery.
   d. were willing to abolish only three-fifths of the slaves.

7. That the Constitution shifted power from the states to the central government is made evident by giving Congress power
   a. to lay and collect taxes.
   b. to regulate foreign and domestic commerce.
   c. to pass all laws "necessary and proper" for carrying out other powers.
   d. all of the above.

8. Jefferson's Bill for Establishing Religious Freedom
   a. was created to end the privilege of Massachusetts Congregationalists.
   b. turned the Church of England into the Episcopal Church.
   c. rejected all connections between church and state, and removed all religious tests for public office.
   d. was based on the First Amendment to the Constitution.

9. All of the following participated in the Constitutional Convention EXCEPT
    a. Thomas Jefferson.
    b. George Washington.
    c. Benjamin Franklin.
    d. James Madison.

10. After the War for Independence, Americans were angry with Spain for
    a. unlawfully occupying all of Florida.
    b. holding most of the post-war debt.
    c. closing the mouth of the Mississippi River to American commerce.
    d. all of the above.

11. Anti-Federalists believed that
    a. the Constitutional Convention was unfortunate but thoroughly legal.
    b. separation of powers was enough to prevent the abuse of power in the new government.
    c. republican liberty was best preserved by the balancing of factions.
    d. republican liberty was best preserved in small, simple, homogeneous societies.

12. Madison argued in *Federalist No. 10* that factions were
    a. necessary to maintaining liberty in a republic.
    b. more likely to destroy liberty in a large republic than in a small one.
    c. undemocratic and therefore should be suppressed.
    d. good for homogeneous states but unnecessary in a federal system.

13. The ratification process revealed that Federalist strength was strongest
    a. in small interior farm regions.
    b. in coastal cities and towns.
    c. in the South except for Georgia.
    d. among merchants but not working-class artisans and workers.

True or False: Questions on the U.S. Constitution

___ 1. The Constitution (plus laws and treaties) is the supreme law of the land.

___ 2. The Constitution created a Supreme Court and 13 district courts.

___ 3. Congress has the power to coin money.

___ 4. Congress may not tax exports.

___ 5. The president makes treaties with the approval of two-thirds of Congress.

___ 6. The president appoints ambassadors, judges, and other officials with the advice and consent of the Senate.

___7. To be a senator, one must be at least 35 years old.

___8. Treason consists of levying war against the United States or giving aid and comfort to the enemy.

___9. Slaves and indentured servants count as three-fifths of a person for purposes of representation.

___10. All bills for raising revenue must originate in the House of Representatives.

___11. New states may be admitted to the Union by Congress.

___12. The United States may intervene against domestic violence within a state.

___13. The president declares war with the approval of two-thirds of Congress.

___14. The phrase "life, liberty, and the pursuit of happiness" from the Declaration of Independence reappears in the Constitution.

___15. The president shares with federal courts the power "to faithfully execute the laws."

___16. Amendments may be proposed by either two-thirds of Congress or the states (in legislatures or conventions) and must be ratified by three-quarters of the states (in legislatures or conventions).

___17. The First Amendment guarantees the rights of speech, press, petition, religion, and bearing of arms.

___18. The president may veto decisions of the Supreme Court.

Essays

1. Explain why the Articles of Confederation were considered too weak for the fledgling republic.

2. Show how the roots of the main provisions of the Constitution are in the colonial experience under English rule as well as in the Articles of Confederation period.

3. To what extent did the Constitution continue or contract revolutionary republicanism?

4. Why did Anti-Federalists want to defeat ratification of the Constitution, and why were they unsuccessful?

Identify and Interpret: Quotation
(that is, state who, what, where, when, and why significant)

*That this is a consolidated government is demonstrably clear; and the danger of such a government is, to my mind, very striking. I have the highest veneration for those gentlemen; but, sir, say, **We, the people**? My political curiosity, exclusive of my anxious solicitude for the public welfare, leads me to ask, Who authorized them to speak the language of **We, the people**, instead of, **We, the states**? States are the characteristics and the soul of a confederation.*

8

Creating a Nation

(1) CHAPTER OUTLINE

David Brown, Revolutionary War veteran, seaman, and pamphleteer, increasingly attacked the central government under the new national constitution in the 1790s. He claimed it was a conspiracy of the rich to exploit farmers, artisans, and other common folk. His inflammatory charges aroused the ire of the federal judiciary, which convicted him of sedition and put him in prison. He was released only after the election of Thomas Jefferson in 1800.

Launching the National Republic
    Beginning the New Government
    The Bill of Rights
    The People Divide
    The Whiskey Rebellion

The Republic in a Threatening World
    The Promise and Peril of the French Revolution
    Democratic Revolutions in Europe and the Atlantic World
    The Democratic-Republican Societies
    Jay's Controversial Treaty

The Political Crisis Deepens
    The Election of 1796
    The War Crisis with France
    The Alien and Sedition Acts
    Local Reverberations
    The Virginia and Kentucky Resolutions
    The "Revolution of 1800"

Restoring American Liberty
    The Jeffersonians Take Control
    Politics and the Federal Courts
    Dismantling the Federalist War Program

Building an Agrarian Nation
    The Jeffersonian Vision
    The Windfall Louisiana Purchase
    Opening the Trans-Mississippi West

A Foreign Policy for the New Nation
  Jeffersonian Principles
  Struggling for Neutral Rights

Conclusion: A Period of Trial and Transition

(2) SIGNIFICANT THEMES AND HIGHLIGHTS

1. As David Brown's story suggests, this chapter presents the turbulent political controversies surrounding the launching of the new government in the 1790s.

2. The struggle to create a nation was marked by the formation of two political parties, Federalists and Democratic-Republicans, and by crises in the young nation's relationships with France and England during the presidential administrations of George Washington and John Adams.

3. Underlying the political controversies of the 1790s, as David Brown's life reveals, were class differences between rich and poor, regional differences between the urban Northeast and the interior West and South, and two conflicting ideological views over issues of power, political equality, and the proper role of central government in a republican society.

4. This chapter also emphasizes the successful transition from Adams' administration to Jefferson's administration. It also examines the attempt of Jeffersonian Republicans to reshape national political life and realize their vision of liberty in an agrarian republic.

5. In the field of foreign affairs, Jeffersonians attempted to fashion policies that would free the nation of entangling alliances with European powers, eliminate foreign troops from American soil, and protect American interests.

(3) LEARNING GOALS

Familiarity with Basic Knowledge

After reading this chapter, you should be able to:

1. Describe the Bill of Rights and its significance.

2. Outline Hamilton's view of the proper role of government, his financial plan, and the fate of each proposal.

3. Explain the major events of George Washington's administration, including the causes of the Whiskey Rebellion.

4. Compare and contrast the principles of the French Revolution and the American Revolution.

71

5. State how the French Revolution divided Americans and contributed to the development of party politics.

6. Describe the social composition, political principles, and activities of the Democratic-Republican societies.

7. Describe the major domestic and foreign crises of the administration of John Adams.

8. Explain three measures Jefferson took to reshape and change the federal government.

9. Explain the reasons why Jefferson believed agricultural life was essential to political liberty.

Practice in Historical Thinking Skills

After reading this chapter, you should be able to:

1. Discuss the disagreement over the role of government in the new nation.

2. Compare and contrast the differing ideological positions and visions of the Federalists and the Democratic-Republicans in the 1790s.

3. Decide whether the election of 1800 was, as Jefferson thought, "a revolution in the principles of our government."

(4) IMPORTANT DATES AND NAMES TO KNOW

1789	George Washington inaugurated as first president Outbreak of the French Revolution
1790	Slave trade outlawed in all states except Georgia and South Carolina Hamilton's "Reports on the Public Credit"
1791	Bill of Rights ratified Whiskey Tax and national bank established Hamilton's "Report on Manufactures"
1792	Washington re-elected
1793	Outbreak of war in Europe Washington's Neutrality Proclamation Jefferson resigns from cabinet Controversy over Citizen Genêt's visit
1794	Whiskey Rebellion in Pennsylvania

1795	Controversy over Jay's Treaty with England
1796	Washington's Farewell Address John Adams elected president
1797	XYZ affair in France
1798	Naturalization Act Alien and Sedition Acts Virginia and Kentucky Resolutions
1798-1800	Undeclared naval war with France
1799	Trials of David Brown and Luther Baldwin
1800	Capital moves to Washington
1801	Thomas Jefferson elected president Judiciary Act New Land Act
1802	Judiciary Act repealed
1803	Louisiana Purchase Napoleonic wars resume
1803-1806	Lewis and Clark expedition
1804	Jefferson reelected
1805-1807	Pike explores the West
1806	Non-Importation Act
1807	Embargo Act *Chesapeake-Leopard* Affair Congress prohibits slave trade

Other Names to Know

James Madison	Thomas Pinckney	John Marshall
Aaron Burr	Foreign Minister Talleyrand	Sacajawea
Toussaint L'Ouverture		

(5) GLOSSARY OF IMPORTANT TERMS

Democratic-Republican societies: popular associations in America that supported the ideals of revolutionary France and became the basis of the Jeffersonian Republican party

federalism: a system where political power is divided between a central (national) government and smaller governmental units called states or provinces

federalists: supporters of the ratification of the Constitution and the shift of power from local and state governments to the central government

Federalists: political party organized in the 1790s under Alexander Hamilton and John Adams dedicated to a strong central government, national power and economic growth, and rule by the wealthy elite

(6) ENRICHMENT IDEAS

1. After reading the Recovering the Past section, find and read foreign visitors' accounts of life in the United States in the 1830s and 1840s. How accurate do you think they were? How would you write about another culture you have seen (or imagined)? What questions would you ask? What limitations would you feel? What cultural assumptions would you bring to your observations?

2. Make a chart contrasting the major ideas, political principles, and social composition of the two emerging political party traditions.

(7) SAMPLE TEST AND EXAMINATION QUESTIONS

Multiple choice: Choose the best answer.

1. The Bill of Rights was
    a. part of the original Constitution.
    b. a leftover from the Articles of Confederation.
    c. a means of creating support for the new government.
    d. opposed because it pandered to people.

2. Alexander Hamilton believed that
    a. power belonged to the people.
    b. that most people had poor judgment.
    c. that the rich were no better than the poor.
    d. none of the above.

3. Alexander Hamilton
    a. was a financial and political conservative.
    b. was forward-looking in his economic programs but politically conservative.
    c. believed in free trade but opposed a protective tariff.
    d. believed in distributing powers equally to both the executive and legislative branches of government.

74

4. The primary objectives of Hamilton's financial program were
   a. to promote agricultural growth in the West.
   b. to establish the country's credit with the French.
   c. to promote commercial expansion overseas.
   d. all of the above.

5. Jefferson believed that
   a. the government should only have powers specifically designated by the Constitution.
   b. Hamilton's programs represented a reasonable solution to the new nation's problems.
   c. the yeoman farmer and the city artisan were the backbone of the republic.
   d. Hamilton's proposal for the bank would hinder the development of commerce and manufacturing.

6. The Whiskey Rebellion was incited by
   a. Revolutionary War veterans still angry about taxation without representation.
   b. western Federalists jealous of Hamilton's power over Washington.
   c. resentful farmers whose livelihood was threatened by the tax on whiskey.
   d. tavernkeepers.

7. The French Revolution
   a. was a radical social revolution.
   b. divided both Europeans and Americans.
   c. offered Americans trading opportunities.
   d. all of the above.

8. The Democratic-Republican societies
   a. supported revolutionary France.
   b. supported American neutrality in the European wars.
   c. were led by common working people.
   d. sought to remove both French and English influence from the United States.

9. Jay's Treaty
   a. succeeded in removing the British from western fur-trading posts.
   b. resolved almost none of America's grievances with England.
   c. provided guarantees against the impressment of American seamen.
   d. opened the West Indies to significant American shipping.

10. John Adams and Thomas Jefferson
    a. had similar ideas on the role of the national government.
    b. were contending for the leadership of the Federalist party.
    c. had been enemies from the time of the Continental Congress.
    d. had divergent ideas about the development of the new nation.

11.   The Alien and Sedition Acts
   a.   nearly succeeded in squelching Jeffersonian criticism of Federalist policies.
   b.   were aimed at advocates of a strong navy.
   c.   were declared unconstitutional by the Supreme Court.
   d.   were attacked by Jefferson but defended in Madison's Virginia Resolutions.

12.   The "Revolution of 1800"
   a.   was the occasion of the passage of the Bill of Rights.
   b.   revealed strong sectional divisions.
   c.   represented yet another Federalist victory.
   d.   was decided definitively in the electoral college.

13.   The Federalists
   a.   had strong support in the South as well as in the North.
   b.   had a strong following among agriculturalists.
   c.   had mainly northern support.
   d.   were so weak no one supported the party.

14.   During Jefferson's administration
   a.   Federalists were jailed for criticizing Jefferson.
   b.   the provisional army was dismantled and defense costs lowered.
   c.   farmers were rewarded for homesteading.
   d.   the navy built a large fleet to protect U.S. trade.

Essays

1.   Compare and contrast the ideological positions and visions of the Federalists and the Jeffersonian Democratic-Republicans in the 1790s.

2.   Analyze and evaluate the reasons for the dominance of Federalist party principles in the 1790s.

3.   Explain the reasons for the rise of political parties in the 1790s.

4.   Explain the importance of Hamilton's plans for future economic growth.

5.   Outline the major difficulties that the French Revolution caused for American foreign policy.

6.   Write an essay on the following statement: "Once in power, the Jefersonian Republicans retreated from many of the positions they had held as the opposition party." Show the extent to which you agree with the statement, and support your position with evidence.

Identify and Interpret: Quotation
(that is, state who, what, where, when, and why significant)

Let us, then, with courage and confidence pursue our own Federal and Republican principles, our attachment to union and representative government. Kindly separated by nature and a wide ocean from the exterminating havoc of one quarter of the globe; too high-minded to endure the degradations of the others; possessing a chosen country, with room enough for our descendants to the thousandth and thousandth generation; entertaining a due sense of our equal right to the use of our own faculties, to the acquisitions of our own industry, to honor and confidence from our fellow-citizens, resulting not from birth, but from our actions and their sense of them; enlightened by a benign religion, professed, indeed, and practiced in various forms . . . with all these blessings, what more is necessary to make us a happy and a prosperous people? Still one thing more, fellow-citizens—a wise and frugal Government, which shall restrain men from injuring one another, shall leave them otherwise free to regulate their own pursuits of industry and improvement, and shall not take from the mouth of labor the bread it has earned. This is the sum of good government, and this is necessary to close the circle of our felicities.

9

Society and Politics in the Early Republic

(1) CHAPTER OUTLINE

Mary and James Harrod carry their children and household possessions away from a difficult life in the Virginia uplands to a more hopeful future in Kentucky. Likewise, two African-Americans, Ben Thompson and Phyllis Sherman, arrive from their former homes to carve out a life in New York's community of free blacks.

A Nation of Regions
   The Northeast
   The South
   Trans-Appalachia
   The Nation's Cities

Indian-White Relations in the Early Republic
   The Goals of Indian Policy
   Strategies of Survival: The Iroquois and Cherokee
   Patterns of Armed Resistance: The Shawnee and Creek

Perfecting a Democratic Society
   The Revolutionary Heritage
   The Evangelical Impulse
   Alleviating Poverty and Distress
   Women's Lives
   Race, Slavery, and the Limits of Reform
   Forming Free Black Communities

The End of Neo-Colonialism
   The War of 1812
   The United States and the Americas

Knitting the Nation Together
   Conquering Distance
   Strengthening American Nationalism
   The Specter of Sectionalism

Politics in Transition
    The Collapse of the Federalist-Jeffersonian Party System
    Women at the Republican Court
    A New Style of Politics

Conclusion: The Passing of an Era

(2) SIGNIFICANT THEMES AND HIGHLIGHTS

1. This chapter focuses on the first three decades of the nineteenth century, a period of intense political activity, religious enthusiasm, economic growth, and westward expansion. The chapter emphasizes the attempts of the Jeffersonian Republicans to reshape national political life and to realize their vision of liberty in an agrarian republic.

2. Though the country was politically united, significant regional differences existed between the rural populations of the Northeast, the South, and the Trans-Appalachian West.

3. During the early republic there were numerous efforts to create a distinctive American social order, one that would support the new republican government.

4. The chapter continues the story of Indian-white relations. Between 1790 and 1820, tribal groups developed strategies of accommodation, resistance, and survival. Some tribes, like the Seneca inspired by Handsome Lake, underwent cultural renewal. Others, like the Cherokee, adopted many of the ways of white society. Still others, like the Shawnee and Creek nations, chose armed resistance. At the same time, the federal government developed policies, based on both humanitarian and territorial concerns, that guided Indian-white relations for the rest of the nineteenth century.

5. In the field of foreign affairs, Jeffersonians attempted to fashion policies that would free the nation of entangling alliances with European powers, eliminate foreign troops from American soil, and protect American maritime interests. Although foreign policy measures were in the short run unsuccessful, as the War of 1812 indicated, the United States soon after stated its unique claim to influence the Western Hemisphere.

(3) LEARNING GOALS

Familiarity with Basic Knowledge

After reading this chapter, you should be able to:

1. Explain the basic features of the different regions in the United States.

2. Show how changing land acts affected settlement of the public domain.

3. Explain the significance of reform efforts and the impact on society.

4. Show the conflicting goals of federal Indian policy.

5. Outline the causes and significance of the War of 1812 and of the Monroe Doctrine.

Practice in Historical Thinking Skills

After reading this chapter, you should be able to:

1. Compare and contrast the survival strategies of the Cherokee, Shawnee, and Creek nations and evaluate how well you think their different strategies worked.

2. Discuss the validity of the American claim that the War of 1812 was the "second War of American Independence."

3. Explain the forces that weakened Jefferson's party.

(4) IMPORTANT DATES AND NAMES TO KNOW

1790	Indian Intercourse Act
1790s	Second Great Awakening begins
1793	Invention of the cotton gin
1794	Battle of Fallen Timbers
1795	Treaty of Greenville
1800	Gabriel's Rebellion
1803	*Marbury* v. *Madison*
1806	National Road begun

1807	Fulton's steamboat *Clermont* launched
1808	James Madison elected president Official end of the slave trade
1811	Battle of Kithtippecanoe
1812	Madison reelected War declared against Great Britain
1813	Battle of Thames
1813-1814	Creek War
1814	Treaty of Ghent Battle of Horseshoe Bend
1814-1815	Hartford Convention
1815	Battle of New Orleans
1816	James Monroe elected president Second Bank of the United States chartered American Colonization Society founded African Methodist Episcopal Church established
1819	Adams-Onis Treaty with Spain *McCulloch* v. *Maryland*
1819-1822	Bank panic and depression
1819-1820	Missouri Compromise
1822	Diplomatic recognition of Latin American republics
1823	Monroe Doctrine proclaimed
1824	John Quincy Adams elected president
1827	Cherokees adopt written constitution

Other Names to Know

John Ross	Tecumseh	Benjamin Banneker
Elskwatawa	Judith Murray	Henry Clay
John Marshall	Richard Allen	

(5) GLOSSARY OF IMPORTANT TERMS

full-blooded: term applied to Indians who had only Indian blood to distinguish them from mixed-blooded Indians

War Hawks: a group of Republican leaders, including Clay and Calhoun, who pressed for a warlike stance toward Great Britain and urged territorial expansion into Canada and Florida

(6) ENRICHMENT IDEAS

1. On an outline map of the United States, trace the route of the Lewis and Clark expedition. Fill in the area acquired in the Louisiana Purchase and trace the Transcontinental Treaty Line of 1819 (Adams-Onis). What conclusions do you draw about the relationship between exploration and expansion? Finally, add Florida, New Orleans, and other important battle sites of the War of 1812.

2. Develop a position paper supporting or rejecting war with Great Britain from the point of view of a member of Congress from the South, the West, and New England. What would be the differences between the positions and specific arguments of the three congressmen?

3. Imagine yourself, like the Harrods, moving into Kentucky or Indiana. Or imagine yourself as Ben Thompson and Phyllis Sherman, free blacks carving out a life in New York. Or imagine yourself a Seneca, Shawnee, or Cherokee young person. In each case, describe your life and feelings.

(7) SAMPLE TEST AND EXAMINATION QUESTIONS

Multiple choice: Choose the best answer.

1. Women on northeastern farms
    a. rarely helped with livestock.
    b. contributed little to the farm economy.
    c. saw their value as domestic labor decline as more men worked for a wage outside the farm.
    d. began to be paid a wage by their fathers or husbands for the farm work they did.

2. In the *Marbury* v. *Madison* decision, Chief Justice Marshall
    a. declared the Maryland law taxing the Second Bank of the United States unconstitutional.
    b. decided in favor of Marbury.
    c. affirmed the principle of exclusive judicial review.
    d. all of the above.

3. Which of the following contributed MOST to the decline of forested area in the northeast?
    a. The need for more wooden fences.
    b. The demand for heating fuel.
    c. The production of potash and turpentine.
    d. The demand for wood planks to build houses.

4. The Second Great Awakening's most important impact was
    a. it encouraged believers to take an interest and perform good works in the community.
    b. its message had little meaning for ordinary people.
    c. it appealed only to women who found new spiritual strength.
    d. it created complex theological ideas.

5. All of the following contributed to cotton becoming "king" in the south EXCEPT
    a. Eli Whitney's invention of the cotton gin.
    b. the limited availability of slave labor.
    c. growing demand for cotton in English and American textile mills.
    d. southern planters' experience in producing and marketing staple crops.

6. The federal government between 1790 and 1820
    a. continued to acquire Native American lands.
    b. wanted to protect Indians from unscrupulous exploitation.
    c. adopted a new treaty strategy.
    d. all of the above.

7. In the Trans-Appalachia west
    a. slavery came to dominate south of the Ohio River.
    b. the population was very similar in terms of race, class, and ethnicity.
    c. the Northwest Ordinance was the law of the land.
    d. was free from speculation in land sales.

8. The most eager calls for war with Great Britain came from
    a. the Federalists.
    b. western and southern Republicans.
    c. New England merchants.
    d. southern planters.

9. A distinctive feature of religious practices during the Second Great Awakening was
   a. a meeting with Native American tribal leaders.
   b. a meeting of the young War Hawks.
   c. the camp meetings.
   d. a prayer meeting often held at agricultural fairs.

10. The Treaty of Ghent
    a. resolved outstanding American differences with Great Britain.
    b. avoided most important areas of dispute.
    c. contained an agreement that the British would stop its impressments policy.
    d. resolved boundary disputes in the Oregon Territory.

11. The Monroe Doctrine
    a. was a policy developed by Americans with the aid of British diplomats.
    b. led to American isolationism in European affairs.
    c. led to immediate American involvement in Latin American affairs.
    d. put fear into the hearts of European diplomats.

12. The leader of Shawnee political and military resistance was
    a. Tecumseh.   c. The Prophet.
    b. Sequoyah.   d. Handsome Lake.

13. Between 1812 and 1828,
    a. the Federalist party collapsed.
    b. the Jeffersonian Republicans evolved into a new political party.
    c. the Anti-Federalist party collapsed.
    d. both (a) and (b) happened.

14. All of the following contributed to a growing sense of American nationalism EXCEPT
    a. the Missouri Compromise.
    b. the War of 1812.
    c. ritual celebrations of Washington's birthday and the Fourth of July.
    d. the Supreme Court decision in *McCullough v. Maryland*.

15. When Jefferson said "This momentous question, like a firebell in the night . . . [has] awakened and filled me with terror," he was referring to
    a. the Monroe Doctrine.   c. Gabriel's rebellion.
    b. the War of 1812.   d. the Missouri question.

Essays

1. Write an essay showing the key differences in the geographic regions (Northeast, South, and West).

2. The War of 1812 was not merely a war against an external foe but stemmed from internal problems as well. Write an essay taking this statement as your starting point.

3. Evaluate the survival strategies of several Native American nations and compare them with the foreign policy strategies of the young United States. Which were more successful, and why do you think so?

4. This chapter examines two seemingly contradictory notions: regionalism and nationalism. Write an essay that examines these two ideas, how they co-existed, and which one you think was more important during the early republic.

5. Discuss the ways in which the lives of African Americans changed during the early republic years based on region and changing economic circumstances.

Map question:

Locate the following on the accompanying map.

1. Louisiana Territory
2. Spanish East Florida
3. Missouri Compromise Line
4. disputed Oregon Territory
5. Battle of Kithtippecanoe
6. New Orleans

7. Transcontinental Treaty Line of 1819
8. areas inhabited by the Shawnee, Cherokee, and Creek nations
9. Gulf Coast areas added during War of 1812
10. site of Constitutional Convention

86

PART THREE (Chapters 10–16)

AN EXPANDING PEOPLE 1820–1877

During the first half of the nineteenth century, a young nation expanded rapidly. As Americans surged west across the Appalachians, secured vast new territories beyond the Mississippi, and, in the 1840s, pushed on to the Pacific Coast, the population soared and became more diverse with the arrival of thousands of immigrants and the inclusion of western Indians and Mexicans. In the East, new modes of production laid the foundation for the material comfort that has come to characterize American life. But expansion sharpened regional differences and resulted in the most devastating conflict the nation ever experienced.

Chapters 10, 11, and 12 cover roughly the same time period, with each chapter complementing the others. Chapter 10, "Economic Transformations in the Northeast and the Old Northwest," investigates the economic and social transformations that affected work, social relations, and the rhythms of everyday life in these two regions. Chapter 11, "Slavery and the Old South," considers the South's distinctive economic and social system, which, based as it was on slavery, raised questions about the special virtue of the nation and the meaning of justice, equality, and freedom. In Chapter 12, "Shaping America in the Antebellum Age," we focus on economic and social changes that sharpened the familiar tension between the individual and society. The election of Andrew Jackson as president marked the advent of the second American party system and a lively political culture rooted in new economic and social conditions. Yet while more white Americans became politically active, they disagreed on the competing claims of liberty and power.

Chapter 13, "Moving West," shows the power of American expansionism and the limited meaning many Americans gave to terms like *liberty* and *equality*. During the decade of the 1840s, war and diplomacy won vast new territories, peopled mostly by Mexicans and Native Americans. As settlers to new frontiers sought to re-create familiar institutions and patterns, these earlier inhabitants found themselves excluded from most of the promises of American life. Territorial expansion illustrated questionable environmental practices, the limitations of political and social ideals, and instigated angry political debates. The expansion of slavery into the West threatened the political balance of power between the North and the South and raised the question of where power and authority lay to decide the future of the West. These questions—which are addressed in Chapters 14, 15, and 16—could not be easily resolved.

Chapter 14, "The Union in Peril," traces the disintegration of the second party system. By 1860, two cultures jostled uneasily in one union, unable to agree on most of the important questions of the day. Chapter 15, "The Union Severed," examines the resulting Civil War and the unanticipated results of the conflict. For example, although the war ended slavery, emancipation itself proved to be problematic. Also unexpected were the transformation of northern and southern society and the new conflicts that emerged. Chapter 16, "The Union Reconstructed," explores how Americans tried to resolve these and the many other dilemmas of the postwar period including questions of reunion and the rights of newly freed slaves.

10

Economic Transformations in the Northeast and the Old Northwest

(1) CHAPTER OUTLINE

Susan Warner's privileged and comfortable life is suddenly destroyed when her father loses most of his fortune in the panic of 1837. As Susan searches for ways to help her family, she discovers the economic possibilities of novel writing. Her books attract readers who find her description of the period's economic and social uncertainties convincing.

Economic Growth
   The Transatlantic Context for Growth
   Factors Fueling Economic Development
   Capital and Government Support
   A New Mentality
   Ambivalence Toward Change
   The Advance of Industrialization
   Environmental Consequences

Early Manufacturing

A New England Textile Town
   Working and Living in a Mill Town
   Female Responses to Work
   The Changing Character of the Workforce
   Factories on the Frontier

Urban Life
   The Process of Urbanization
   Class Structure in the Cities
   The Urban Working Class
   Middle-Class Life and Ideals
   Mounting Urban Tensions
   The Black Underclass

Rural Communities
   Farming in the East
   Frontier Families
   Opportunities in the Old Northwest
   Agriculture and the Environment

Conclusion: The Character of Progress

(2) SIGNIFICANT THEMES AND HIGHLIGHTS

1. This chapter concentrates on the economic and social transformations in the Northeast and the Midwest between 1820 and 1860. The chapter discusses the factors contributing to economic growth, particularly the importance of changes in transportation, and explores industrialization as a new means of production and as a source of social change. The chapter shows that the process of industrialization was uneven, as old and new ways of production existed side by side.

2. Five types of communities (Lowell; Philadelphia; Cincinnati; Hampshire County, Massachusetts; and the Indiana frontier) are discussed to show how each participated in economic growth. The ways in which different classes, ethnic groups, and races responded to new conditions and shared or failed to share in the benefits of growth are highlighted.

3. The persistence of Revolutionary ideology is evident in working-class critiques of the new industrial world, while new middle-class ideals emerged as a response to changing economic and social conditions.

4. Samuel Breck of Philadelphia is introduced as an example of an upper-class urban dweller. Several mill girls (Mary Paul and Sally Rice) appear at various points in the chapter. The Skinners give an idea of life on the Indiana frontier.

(3) LEARNING GOALS

Familiarity with Basic Knowledge

After reading this chapter, you should be able to:

1. List and explain major factors contributing to economic growth and explain how changes in transportation were of critical importance.

2. Define the term *industrialization* and identify the parts of the United States where industrialization took hold between 1830 and 1860.

3. Define *separate spheres* and explain the reasons for its development, its flexibility, and its effects on middle-class life.

4. Describe urban class structure and compare it to rural class structure.

5. Explain the process of establishing a family farm on the midwestern frontier.

6. Discuss the contribution of nontangible factors to economic growth.

Practice in Historical Thinking Skills

After reading this chapter, you should be able to:

1. Show how Cincinnati illustrates the uneven process of industrialization and the emergence of new types of work and new workers, and contrast the situation in Cincinnati with the Lowell system.

2. Analyze the ways in which both male and female workers used Revolutionary ideology as a means of criticizing the new work order.

3. Summarize the ways in which economic and social changes affected people's lives both by increasing opportunities and benefits and by separating people from one another.

(4) IMPORTANT DATES AND NAMES TO KNOW

1805	*Palmer* v. *Mulligan*
1816	Second Bank of the United States chartered
1817	New York Stock Exchange established
1819	*Dartmouth College* v. *Woodward*
1820	Land Act of 1820 The expression "woman's sphere" becomes current
1823	City of Lowell, Massachusetts, founded by Boston Associates
1824	*Sturges* v. *Crowninshield*
1824-1850	Construction of canals in the Northeast
1825-1856	Construction of canals linking the Ohio, the Mississippi, and the Great Lakes
1828	Baltimore & Ohio Railroad begins operation
1830	Preemption Act facilitates western land acquisition by squatters
1830s	Boom in the Old Northwest Increasing discrimination against free blacks Public education movement spreads
1833	Philadelphia establishes small police force

1834	Philadelphia race riots
	Lowell work stoppage
	Cyrus McCormick patents his reaper

1837   Horace Mann becomes secretary of Massachusetts Board of Education

1837-1844   Financial panic and depression

1840   Agitation for 10-hour day

1840s-1850s   Rising tide of immigration
     Expansion of railroad system

1844   Anti-Catholic riots in Philadelphia

1849   Cholera epidemic in New York, St. Louis, and Cincinnati

1850s   Rise of urban police forces

1857   Financial Panic

Other Names to Know

Sarah Hale   Catharine Beecher   Prudence Crandall

(5) GLOSSARY OF IMPORTANT TERMS

cult of domesticity: set of beliefs insisting that women had different characteristics than men, which made them best suited for the private sphere of home and family

economic growth: an increase in output, usually involving not only expansion but changes in the methods of production

entrepreneur: one who takes the risks of starting new ventures or one who owns or manages one or more businesses

industrial mode of production: the reorganization of production, breaking the process into a series of separate steps done by individual workers or machines

outwork: work done at home or in small shops; workers were usually paid by the piece

Waltham system: the system of textile production in which all stages of the manufacturing process were brought together

(6) ENRICHMENT IDEAS

1. Using the Recovering the Past section as your guide, explore some volumes of early nineteenth-century paintings. What can you discover about the nature of daily life, attitudes, and values from your study?

2. Think how you might write an article for a Cincinnati newspaper evaluating some of the changes in work in the antebellum period if you were the owner of a furniture factory, a widow taking in piecework, or a former cabinetmaker now working in the factory.

3. Write a diary entry for one day in the life of a Lowell mill girl in the 1830s. Give a clear sense of your daily schedule as well as your response to your job and free time. How would your entry differ if you were an Irish girl in the 1850s?

4. If you live in the Midwest, visit the Conner Prairie Settlement near Indianapolis. This living-history museum, which uses first-person interpreters as villagers, conveys a realistic picture of daily life on the frontier in the 1830s. Other living museums can suggest the ways in which rural American life changed in the period before the Civil War.

5. If you live in or near a northeastern, Middle Atlantic, or South Atlantic city, plan a walking tour to the part of the city constructed during the period covered by this chapter. What kinds of buildings date from that era? What were they used for? Are there any examples of housing? What class of persons may have lived in these houses? Are there any remaining evidences of working-class neighborhoods? Visit an early mill complex. What can it tell you about the industrial process, the nature of work, and the reality of life in a mill community?

(7) SAMPLE TEST AND EXAMINATION QUESTIONS

Multiple choice: Choose the best answer.

1. The Lowell work force was typically made up of
    a. older married women.
    b. married men.
    c. single men.
    d. young single women.

2. Lowell mill owners constructed boardinghouses for their workers because
    a. they believed workers needed comfortable housing.
    b. they wanted to attract a respectable work force.
    c. they believed privacy was essential after a long day of toil.
    d. they were copying European models.

3. Between 1820 and 1840, the percentage of Americans living in cities
   a. stayed about the same.
   b. approximately doubled.
   c. barely increased.
   d. decreased by almost half.

4. Population growth in the early decades of the nineteenth century occurred because of
   a. the increasing size of families.
   b. a dramatic drop in death rates.
   c. an increase in foreign immigration, mainly from Ireland and Germany.
   d. an increase in immigrants from eastern and southern Europe.

5. State governments
   a. rarely gave economic entrepreneurs special advantages.
   b. levied heavy taxes on business profits.
   c. favored farmers.
   d. gave loans for internal improvements.

6. In relation to economic growth, the courts
   a. were slow to recognize new attitudes toward property.
   b. established the basic principle that contracts were binding.
   c. were lenient toward debtors.
   d. none of the above.

7. Early textile mills clustered around waterways in
   a. the South.
   b. only New England.
   c. the Middle Atlantic states.
   d. in New England and the Middle Atlantic states.

8. The Erie Canal connected
   a. the Great Lakes with New York's Hudson River.
   b. the Great Lakes with the Mississippi River.
   c. Lake Erie with Lake Ontario.
   d. all of the above.

9. The composition of the Lowell work force changed because
   a. women got married and therefore did not need the money.
   b. women found they could earn more in other jobs.
   c. mill owners preferred to hire Irish immigrants, who worked for less.
   d. unions successfully organized the mills.

10. The idea of separate spheres suggested
   a. that while men and women were substantially similar, women belonged in the private sphere.
   b. that women should make vital economic contributions to their families.
   c. that women's innate differences from men made them suitable only for the private sphere.
   d. that women belonged in the public sphere.

11. Most Cincinnati workers labored
   a. alone.
   b. in small and medium-size shops.
   c. in large factories.
   d. alongside slaves.

12. City services in northern cities were generally provided for
   a. all citizens.
   b. all white citizens.
   c. all but the Irish.
   d. those who could pay for them.

13. Between 1830 and 1860,
   a. the gap between the urban rich and the poor narrowed.
   b. many of the poor entered the middle class.
   c. the gap between rich and poor widened.
   d. little changed.

14. Rural Americans in the Northeast
   a. had little contact with new economic trends.
   b. were born, raised, and died in the same communities.
   c. began to change traditional patterns as they came into contact with the industrial world.
   d. generally enjoyed social and economic equality.

15. Many Americans believed that free public education was important because
   a. they wanted their children to be independent thinkers.
   b. it inculcated proper work habits.
   c. it promoted social change.
   d. it was a good way to keep children off the street.

16. Horace Mann was
   a. an educational reformer.
   b. an early manufacturer of textiles.
   c. an inventor of railroad equipment.
   d. a Philadelphia banker.

17. The 1834 riots in Philadelphia resulted from all of the following EXCEPT
    a. urban expansion.
    b. the existence of black affluence.
    c. a large and over-zealous police force.
    d. competition between poor whites and poor blacks for jobs.

Identify and show a relationship between each of the following pairs:

falling birth rates	*and*	new views of childhood
Lowell mills	*and*	Philadelphia
Irish immigration	*and*	frontier farming
Philadelphia race riot	*and*	Lowell work stoppage of 1834
cult of domesticity	*and*	*Dartmouth* v. *Woodward*

Essays

1. Items 1–3 under "Practice in Historical Thinking Skills" in "Learning Goals" suggest topics for practice in essay writing.

2. The life of "intimacy and quietness" was disintegrating in the decades between 1830 and 1860 and was replaced by a life of separateness and clamor. Discuss this statement with appropriate supporting evidence.

Identify and Interpret: Quotation
(that is, state who, what, where, when, and why significant)

Rules and Regulations to be attended to and followed by the Young Persons who come to Board in this House:

Rule first: *Each one to enter the house without unnecessary noise or confusion, and hang up their bonnet, shawl, coat, etc., in the entry.*

Rule second: *Each one to have their place at the table during meals, the two which have worked the greatest length of time in the Factory to sit on each side of the head of the table, so that all new hands will of course take their seats lower down, according to the length of time they have been here.*

Rule third: *It is expected that order and good manners will be preserved at table during meals – and at all other times either upstairs or down.*

Rule fourth: *There is no unnecessary dirt to be brought into the house by the Boarders, such as apple cores or peels, or nut shells, etc.*

Rule fifth: *Each boarder is to take her turn in making the bed and sweeping the chamber in which she sleeps. . . .*

Rule eighth: *The doors will be closed at ten o'clock at night, winter and summer, at which time each boarder will be expected to retire to bed.*

Rule ninth: *Sunday being appointed by our Creator as a Day of Rest and Religious Exercises, it is expected that all boarders will have sufficient discretion as to pay suitable attention to the day, and . . . they will keep within doors and improve their time in reading, writing, and in other valuable and harmless employment.*

11

Slavery and the Old South

(1) CHAPTER OUTLINE

Frederick Douglass learns from his masters about complex, intricate chains that bind slaves and masters to each other. He also learns that education is the way to freedom.

Building a Diverse Cotton Kingdom
  The Expansion of Slavery in a Global Economy
  Slavery in Latin America
  White and Black Migrations in the South
  Southern Dependence on Slavery
  Paternalism and Honor in the Planter Class
  Slavery, Class, and Yeoman Farmers
  The Nonslaveholding South

Morning: Master and Mistress in the Big House
  The Burdens of Slaveholding
  The Plantation Mistress
  Justifying Slavery

Noon: Slaves in House and Fields
  Daily Toil
  Slave Health and Punishments
  Slave Law and the Family

Night: Slaves in Their Quarters
  Black Christianity
  The Power of Song
  The Enduring Family

Resistance and Freedom
  Forms of Black Protest
  Slave Revolts
  Free Blacks: Becoming One's Own Master

Conclusion: Douglass's Dream of Freedom

(2) SIGNIFICANT THEMES AND HIGHLIGHTS

1. The tremendous growth of agriculture in the Old South was dependent on cotton and slavery. But contrary to myth, the South was an area of great diversity, regionally, socially, and in terms of class and slave ownership. These differences bred tensions among whites as well as between masters and slaves.

2. Although slavery was a labor system, the chapter emphasizes the daily life and complex, entangled relationships of white masters and black slaves and points out the difficulties of generalizing about their relationships. The experiences of the family of rice planter Robert Allston suggests some of the dimensions of white slaveholders' lives, while the youth of Frederick Douglass illuminates the lives of black slaves.

3. A unique structure in this chapter discusses slavery in three sections: morning in the Big House, which focuses on white masters; noon in the fields, which looks at daily work and other hardships of the slaves; and nighttime in the quarters, which describes a slave culture and community centered around religion, music, the family, and other adaptive survivals from African culture.

4. Racism was not confined to the South but existed throughout American society. Racism as well as slavery limited black freedom. To a much lesser extent, southern slaveholders also suffered limitations on their freedom from the burdens of the slave system.

(3) LEARNING GOALS

Familiarity with Basic Knowledge

After reading this chapter, you should be able to:

1. Distinguish several geographic regions and the main crops; then describe the socioeconomic class variations of slaveholding patterns in the Old South.

2. Explain the distribution of slaveholders and nonslaveholders in the South.

3. Describe the burdens of slavery from the perspective of the slaveholders and explain five ways in which they justified slavery.

4. Describe a typical day on the plantation for slave men and women, both in the house and in the fields.

5. Explain the nature of black family life and culture in the slave quarters, including how religion, music, and folklore gave the slaves a sense of identity and self-esteem.

6. List five ways in which the slaves protested and resisted their situation.

Practice in Historical Thinking Skills

After reading this chapter, you should be able to:

1. Develop arguments for and against slavery from the perspective of southern slaveholders, nonslaveholding southerners, northern whites, slaves, and freed blacks.

2. Discuss and evaluate the question of who was "free" in southern antebellum society.

3. Identify the author's interpretation of slavery and other possible interpretations.

(4) IMPORTANT DATES AND NAMES TO KNOW

1787	Constitution adopted with proslavery provisions
1793	Eli Whitney invents cotton gin
1800	Gabriel conspiracy in Virginia
1808	External slave trade prohibited by Congress
1820	South becomes world's largest cotton producer
1822	Denmark Vesey's conspiracy in Charleston
1830s	Southern justification of slavery changes from a necessary evil to a positive good
1831	Nat Turner's slave revolt in Virginia
1845	*Narrative of the Life of Frederick Douglass* published
1850s	Cotton boom
1851	Indiana state constitution excludes free blacks
1852	Harriet Beecher Stowe publishes best-selling *Uncle Tom's Cabin*
1860	Cotton production and prices peak

Other Names to Know

Robert and Adele Allston	Harriet Jacobs	Sophia and Hugh Auld
George Fitzhugh	Maria Stewart	Reverend J. C. Pennington
Harriet Tubman		

(5) GLOSSARY OF IMPORTANT TERMS

culture: the values and way of life of a group of people that gives the group a unifying identity

Herrenvolk democracy: the theory in the antebellum South that although there were economic inequalities among whites, all whites still shared an equality in their superiority to all blacks, a theory that enabled the southern planter elite to minimize class antagonisms among whites

manumission: the freeing of slaves by individual owners

polygenesis: the belief that blacks were a separately created race and hence inherently inferior

(6) ENRICHMENT IDEAS

1. Find more folktales and stories told by slaves and analyze what they reveal about slave culture. See Harold Courlander, *A Treasury of Afro-American Folklore* (1976) or J. Mason Brewer, *American Negro Folklore* (1968).

2. Listen to some slave spirituals and work songs and analyze them. What do they reveal about the slave experience and about attitudes toward religion? Notice the double meanings.

3. Are there any historical sites in your area related to slavery—for example, plantations, stations on the underground railroad, or slave markets? Do restored plantations give a balanced view of life on the old plantation, the slave quarters as well as the Big House?

4. Consider the heritage of slavery in modern society. To what extent does it still affect our lives and how?

5. Are blacks and whites more or less "free" today than they were during slavery? Are they more or less entangled with each other?

(7) SAMPLE TEST AND EXAMINATION QUESTIONS

Multiple choice: Choose the best answer.

1. Most southern families had
   a. fewer than ten slaves.
   b. over ten slaves.
   c. no slaves.
   d. fewer than five slaves.

2. The "black belt" refers to
   a. whips used by slave-drivers to punish unruly slaves.
   b. the Upper South of Virginia and Kentucky.
   c. southern cities.
   d. the deep southern states stretching from South Carolina westward to Texas.

3. What percentage of southern white families were slaveholders?
   a. 25 percent.
   b. 50 percent.
   c. 75 percent.
   d. 90 percent.

4. The most valuable export crop in the South was
   a. cotton.
   b. corn.
   c. rice.
   d. tobacco.

5. All of the following are true of the internal slave trade EXCEPT
   a. it was multimillion-dollar industry.
   b. it was outlawed in 1808 by Congress.
   c. it tended to move slaves from the upper south to the deep south.
   d. attempts at controlling it were poorly enforced.

6. Most slaves worked
   a. in agriculture.
   b. as domestic servants.
   c. as artisans.
   d. in factories.

7. Slaves working the fields
   a. commonly worked 14 hour days during the summer.
   b. preferred gang labor to task labor.
   c. had diversified diets.
   d. were given adequate clothing.

8. The sociological justification of slavery based its argument primarily on
   a. the Bible.
   b. the Constitution.
   c. assumptions about black inferiority and savagery.
   d. history.

9. After Nat Turner's revolt in 1831, slaves were
   a. more easily given their freedom but treated more harshly.
   b. feared even more by whites in the South.
   c. given more education and religious training.
   d. given the right to vote.

10. Which of the following statements is not true about slave women?
    a. they had networks for mutual support.
    b. they were encouraged to have many children.
    c. they had no choice in their marriage partners.
    d. they sometimes resisted forcible sexual encounters by whites.

11. African forms of religious expression
    a. gradually died out in the New World.
    b. were too sinful to survive in civilized society.
    c. survived in adapted form in the New World.
    d. survived in the West Indies but not in the United States.

12. The slave family
    a. was destroyed by the slave trade.
    b. played a key role in achieving black self-esteem.
    c. imitated the family patterns of whites.
    d. transmitted black family patterns to whites.

13. By the 1850s, the largest number of free blacks were in
    a. the North.
    b. the Upper South.
    c. the Lower South.
    d. Canada.

14. All of the following were examples of day-to-day resistance by slaves EXCEPT
    a. breaking tools.
    b. armed revolt.
    c. feigning illness.
    d. arson.

15. All of the following were true of slave religion EXCEPT
    a. it was a means of social control when ministered by whites.
    b. some slaves sought "earthly liberty" from Christian messages.
    c. very few slaves attended any religious services.
    d. it mixed Christian, Islamic, and African traditions.

16. Urban free blacks
    a. often owned their own black slaves.
    b. were generally young.
    c. built community institution like churches, schools and benevolent societies.
    d. Were less likely to be mulattoes compared to the general slave population.

Identify and show a relationship between each of the following pairs:

James Hammond	*and*	Newton Knight
Frederick Douglass	*and*	Sophia Auld
yeoman farmers	*and*	poor whites
Christianity	*and*	slave families
day-to-day resistance	*and*	Nat Turner's revolt

Essays

1. Describe four class levels of southern white society, and show how each might have defended or justified slavery as necessary or good for its self-interest. Which would have defended slavery most vigorously, and why do you think so?

2. Compare and contrast some of the typical events in the daily life of a house slave and a field slave. Which would you have preferred to be and why?

3. Discuss the institution of slavery in a global context. Consider the global economy and the institution itself in Latin America and the United States.

4. Compare and contrast the attitudes of white southerners and white northerners toward blacks. How do you explain whatever differences seem to exist?

5. Describe four or five manifestations of slave culture. Be as specific as you can about sources and modes of expression. Which do you think best expressed authentic slave culture and why?

6. Present an interpretation of slavery from the point of view of three different historians. One sees slavery from the perspective of southern slaveholders, one from the viewpoint of northern white abolitionists, and one from the perspective of the slaves themselves. What would be the major differences?

7. Explain the living conditions, economic circumstances, and day-to-day life that prevailed for non-slaveholding southern farm families.

12

Shaping America in the Antebellum Age

(1) CHAPTER OUTLINE

Emily and Marius Robinson are separated shortly after their marriage because of their ardent commitment to abolish slavery and to educate free blacks. Despite suffering many hardships of separation, sickness, and mob attack, they persist for a time in an effort to shape and reform American society.

Religious Revival and Reform Philosophy
    Finney and the Second Great Awakening
    The Transcendentalists

The Political Response to Change
    Changing Political Culture
    Jackson's Path to the White House
    Old Hickory's Vigorous Presidency
    Jackson's Native American Policy
    Jackson's Bank War and "Van Ruin's" Depression
    The Second American Party System

Perfectionist Reform and Utopianism
    The International Character of Reform
    The Dilemmas of Reform
    Utopian Communities: Oneida and the Shakers
    Other Utopias
    Millerites and Mormons

Reforming Society
    Temperance
    Health and Sexuality
    Humanizing the Asylum
    Working-Class Reform

Abolitionism and Women's Rights
    Tensions Within the Antislavery Movement
    Flood Tide of Abolitionism
    Women Reformers and Women's Rights

Conclusion: Perfecting America

(2) SIGNIFICANT THEMES AND HIGHLIGHTS

1. The social and economic changes of the 1830s were both promising and unsettling. This chapter explores the question of how people (both ordinary and prominent) sought to maintain some sense of control over their lives in the 1830s and 1840s. Some, like the Robinsons, poured their energies into reform. Others turned to politics, religion, and new communal lifestyles in order to shape their changing world.

2. Throughout the chapter, social, political, cultural, and economic topics are interrelated and seen as a whole. The chapter merges two major events—democratic Jacksonian politics and the many forms of perfectionist social reform. They began from distinctly different points of view but in fact shared more in common than has usually been recognized.

3. The explanation of politics in the age of Jackson looks at the social and ethnocultural basis of politics, while the analysis of revivalism, religion, and utopian communitarianism stresses the socioeconomic basis of these cultural phenomena.

4. The timeless dilemmas and problems of reformers, especially of temperance, abolitionist, and feminist reformers, are a sub-theme running through the chapter.

(3) LEARNING GOALS

Familiarity with Basic Knowledge

After reading this chapter, you should be able to:

1. Explain the connection between religious revivalism and reform efforts to erase social evils.

2. Describe three ways in which political culture changed between the early 1820s and 1840.

3. Explain the key events and significance of three major issues in Jackson's presidency—the tariff, the war against the bank, and Indian removal.

4. List and explain the leaders, principles, programs, and sources of support of the two major parties, Democrats and Whigs.

5. List several evils that Americans wanted to reform in the 1830s and 1840s and the major influences that contributed to the reform impulse.

6. Describe some of the purposes, patterns, and problems that most utopian communities shared.

7. Describe the major goals, tactics, and problems in the antebellum reform movements for temperance, abolitionism, and women's rights.

Practice in Historical Thinking Skills

After reading this chapter, you should be able to:

1. Analyze how Jacksonian politicians and social reformers both opposed one another and had much in common.

2. Explain how the changing numbers and composition of voters affected the political structure.

3. Explain the development of the second American party system, showing how it evolved from and differed from the first party system.

4. Understand and explain why people turn to politics, or to religion and revivalism, or to utopian communitarianism, or to specific issue reforms in order to shape their world; and then explain how well these seemed to work.

(4) IMPORTANT DATES AND NAMES TO KNOW

1824	New Harmony established
1825	John Quincy Adams chosen president by the House of Representatives
1826	American Temperance Society founded
1828	Calhoun publishes *Exposition and Protest* Jackson defeats Adams for the presidency Tariff of Abominations
1828-1832	Rise of workingmen's parties
1830	Webster-Hayne debate and Jackson-Calhoun toast Joesph Smith, *The Book of Mormon* Indian Removal Act
1830-1831	Charles Finney's religious revivals
1831	Garrison begins publishing *The Liberator*
1832	Jackson vetoes U.S. Bank charter Jackson re-elected *Worcester* v. *Georgia*
1832-1833	Nullification crisis
1832-1836	Removal of funds from U.S. Bank to state banks

1833	Force Bill
	Calhoun resigns as vice president
	American Anti-Slavery Society founded
1834	New York Female Moral Reform Society founded
	National Trades Union founded
	Whig party established
1835-1836	Countless incidents of mob violence
1836	"Gag rule"
	Specie Circular
	Van Buren elected president
1837	Financial panic and depression
	Sarah Grimké, *Letters on the Condition of Women and the Equality of the Sexes*
1837-1838	Cherokee "Trail of Tears"
1840	William Henry Harrison elected president
	American Anti-Slavery Society splits
	World Anti-Slavery Convention
	10-hour day for federal employees
	Liberty party formed
1840-1841	Transcendentalists found Hopedale and Brook Farm
1843	Dorothea Dix's report on treatment of the insane
1844	Joseph Smith murdered in Nauvoo, Illinois
1846-1848	Mormon migration to the Great Basin
1847	First issue of Frederick Douglass's *North Star*
1848	Oneida community founded
	First women's rights convention at Seneca Falls, New York
1850	Nathaniel Hawthorne's *Scarlet Letter* is published
1851	Maine prohibition law
	Herman Melville's *Moby Dick* is published
1853	Children's Aid Society established in New York City
1854	Thoreau's *Walden* is published
1855	Massachusetts bans segregated public schools

Other Names to Know

Henry Clay	Daniel Webster	Nicholas Biddle
Alexis de Tocqueville	Charles G. Finney	Mother Ann Lee
Robert Owen	Brigham Young	William Miller
Elizabeth Cady Stanton	Theodore Dwight Weld	Abby Kelley
Sylvester Graham	Sojourner Truth	David Walker
Margaret Fuller	Henry Highland Garnet	Lucretia Mott
Ralph Waldo Emerson		

(5) GLOSSARY OF IMPORTANT TERMS

abolitionists: reformers who wanted to end slavery

communitarianism: the creation of utopian communities in which members engaged in various forms of cooperation and sharing of property and responsibility for the well-being of all

ethnocultural politics: the belief that political participation and behavior are affected by one's religious, ethnic, and cultural background

immediatists: abolitionist disciples of Garrison and Weld who wanted to end slavery immediately

nonresistance: the philosophical pacifist belief opposing all forms of governmental or personal coercion

nullification: the states' rights doctrine presented by John C. Calhoun of South Carolina which said that a state could declare federal legislation null and void

perfectionism: the religious belief that sin and evil could be eradicated in American society as well as in individuals

spiritualism: psychic phenomenon of the 1830s and 1840s by which humans believed they could communicate with unknown worlds, including the dead

transcendentalism: belief of New England intellectuals that the truths found beyond sense experience in intuition and nature would lead people to self-knowledge and self-reliance and ultimately to the attempted reformation of themselves and society

Whigs: party opposing Jackson ("King Andrew I"), their name referring to the English parliamentary party opposed to royal power

(6) ENRICHMENT IDEAS

1. After reading the Recovering the Past section, find and read slave narrative accounts of slave life in the United States during the antebellum period. How valid are slave narratives as historical sources? How accurate do you think they were? How would you write about another culture you have seen (or imagined)? What questions would you ask?

2. Visit the site of one of the several utopian communities mentioned in the chapter. Many still exist, some even restored as living historical museums. Depending on where you live, you might visit Hopedale or Brook Farm near Boston, Massachusetts; Shaker Villages near Pittsfield, Massachusetts and in Kentucky; Ephrata, Pennsylvania; Zoar, Ohio; New Harmony, Indiana; the Amana colonies in Iowa, etc. Whether or not you can actually visit the original site, you can research further into one or two particular utopian communities.

3. Imagine yourself as part of the colony. How well would you fit in? What would you like and dislike about life in this community? Write a letter to a friend about it, or write a series of imaginary diary entries about life in the community.

4. You can think about similar questions when visiting other sites, for example, Seneca Falls, or Mormon landmarks in Utah, or a prison asylum built in the mid-nineteenth century. A letter or diary entry could be written about your imagined participation in a Whig campaign picnic in 1840, or a revival or temperance meeting broken up by a mob, or a meeting of Mormons considering migration westward, or your presence at the women's rights convention in Seneca Falls.

5. Prepare a diagram showing the development of the American political party system from the 1790s to 1840—specifically party names, leaders, principles, programs, campaign issues, and sources of popular electoral support.

(7) SAMPLE TEST AND EXAMINATION QUESTIONS

Multiple choice: Choose the best answer.

1. The Whig party stood for all of the following programs EXCEPT
   a. a strong national bank.
   b. a high protective tariff.
   c. state and local autonomy.
   d. restrictions on Sunday business and drinking.

2. Which of the following statements best describes the tone of Jackson's presidency?
   a. The emergence of common people to responsibility in government.
   b. Strong presidential leadership on issues and positions of personal importance to Jackson.
   c. Unyielding presidential leadership to the principles long clearly identified with the Democratic party.
   d. Negative leadership, relying on the "kitchen cabinet" to run most executive affairs.

3. Jackson defeated John Quincy Adams in 1828 because
    a. Clay's candidacy split the votes Adams should have received.
    b. Adams was such an intellectual that the voters did not understand him.
    c. voters were so outraged at the attacks on Rachel Jackson that many voted against Adams.
    d. Jackson carefully prepared for the election, building a sectionally diverse coalition of support.

4. Jacksonian Democrats
    a. supported the concentration of economic power in new corporations.
    b. opposed federal government support for internal improvements.
    c. were basically advocates of national rather than state sovereignty.
    d. encouraged abolitionist criticisms of slavery.

5. The Jacksonian era was noteworthy for which change in political practice?
    a. Fewer men participated by voting.
    b. Party organization helped to promote a more democratic style.
    c. Women began to vote in state elections.
    d. Only wealthy people could afford to run for office.

6. The U.S. Bank performed all of the following services EXCEPT
    a. shifting government funds to different parts of the country
    b. moderating and regulating state banking activities
    c. issuing large quantities of paper money to stimulate purchasing power
    d. buying and selling government bonds

7. The nullification crisis was resolved when
    a. Jackson sent federal troops to Charleston.
    b. popular support for Jackson's threat of force and the compromise tariff isolated South Carolina.
    c. Calhoun apologized and resigned as vice-president.
    d. Van Buren secured passage of the Tariff of Abominations.

8. The removal of the Cherokee Indians was justified by all of the following EXCEPT
    a. Jackson's argument that the Cherokee could not survive living among whites.
    b. Jackson's argument that they were subject to Georgia state laws.
    c. John Marshall's argument that the Indian's case was "repugnant to the Constitution."
    d. white Georgians' arguments that they needed more land for cotton.

9. Which one did not support the Whig party?
    a. New England.
    b. Small Catholic farmers.
    c. Temperance and other moralistic reformers.
    d. Large cotton planters with a national vision.

10. The primary cause of the reform impulse in America in the 1830s was
    a. the influx of Catholic European immigrants.
    b. religious revivalism and socioeconomic changes.
    c. northern opposition to slavery.
    d. an outpouring of new books describing Biblical scriptures.

11. The Finney revivals were characterized by
    a. the idea that ministers were agents who could cause a revival.
    b. the idea that revivals were signs of divine intervention.
    c. extensive drinking during the lengthy meetings.
    d. an emphasis on reason in seeing one's way to conversion.

12. Utopian communities collapsed for all of the following reasons EXCEPT
    a. individualism.
    b. poor leadership and admissions policies.
    c. external hostility.
    d. diversified economies.

13. Black and white abolitionists
    a. did not work well together because of white paternalism.
    b. supported each other well despite occasional disagreements.
    c. worked together only in battling race discrimination in the North but not slavery in the South.
    d. ignored each other because of the fear of mob violence.

14. Which one was not a concern of the women's rights movement in the 1840s?
    a. The right to vote.
    b. The right of free speech.
    c. Better working conditions.
    d. Equal pay for equal work.

15. Temperance reformers
    a. focused exclusively on the moral suasion tactic that drinking was a sin.
    b. were split between advocates of moderation and total abstinence.
    c. succeeded in passing a prohibition amendment before the Civil War.
    d. were led by women who hoped to leave abusive husbands.

Matching:

Match the person in column A with the appropriate religious or reform concern in column B.

A	B
____1. Dorothea Dix	a. antislavery and women's rights
____2. William Miller	b. Oneida colony
____3. Abby Kelley	c. public education
____4. Theodore Dwight Weld	d. Shakers
____5. David Ruggles	e. treatment of the insane
____6. Martin Delany	f. abolitionism and temperance
____7. Ralph Waldo Emerson	g. excessive federal power
____8. Horace Mann	h. secular utopian communities
____9. Sylvester Graham	i. black nationalist colonization
___10. Joseph Smith	j. northern racial discrimination
___11. John H. Noyes	k. *Walden*
___12. Robert Owen	l. Second Coming of Christ
___13. Ann Lee	m. diet and sexual restraint
___14. Henry David Thoreau	n. self-reliance
___15. John C. Calhoun	o. Mormonism

Essays

1. Trace the changing development of the American political party system (and political culture) from 1824 to 1840.

2. Discuss the various dilemmas and problems of reformers, with specific references to the temperance, abolitionist, and women's rights movements.

3. Show the relationship between women's rights and abolitionism.

4. Discuss both the differences and the similarities of Jacksonian politics and social reform.

5. Discuss the many reasons why Americans in the 1830s turned to religion, revivalism, utopianism, and reform. Which approach do you think brought individuals the most satisfaction that they had effectively reshaped their world? Did any? Support your essay with evidence from the chapter.

Identify and Interpret: Quotation
(that is, state who, what, where, when, and why significant)

The history of mankind is a history of repeated injuries and usurpations on the part of man toward woman, having in direct object the establishment of an absolute tyranny over her. To prove this, let facts be submitted to a candid world.

He has never permitted her to exercise her inalienable right to the elective franchise.

He has compelled her to submit to laws, in the formation of which she had no voice.

He has withheld from her rights which are given to the most ignorant and degraded men—both natives and foreigners.

Identify and Interpret: Chart

(that is, first, study the chart and describe what it shows; second, analyze the chart by explaining some of the reasons behind the patterns you see; third, assess the larger significance of the chart)

Public Land Sales, 1820-1860

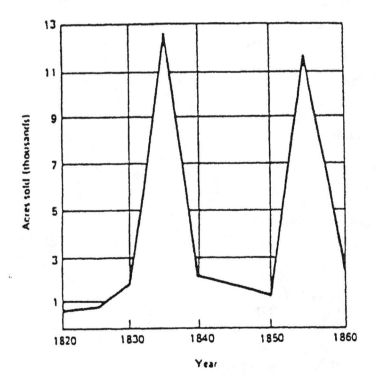

113

13

Moving West

(1) CHAPTER OUTLINE

Narcissa Whitman and her husband Marcus, were among thousands of Americans who played a part in the movement into the trans-Mississippi West between 1830 and 1865. The chapter also examines responses of Native Americans and Mexican Americans to expansion and illuminates the different ways cultural traditions intersected in the West.

Probing the Trans-Mississippi West
    The International Context for American Expansionism
    Early Interest in the West
    Manifest Destiny

Winning the Trans-Mississippi West
    Annexing Texas, 1845
    War with Mexico, 1846–1848
    California and New Mexico
    The Treaty of Guadalupe Hidalgo, 1848
    The Oregon Question, 1844–1846

Going West and East
    The Emigrants
    Migrants' Motives
    The Overland Trails

Living in the West
    Farming in the West
    Mining Western Resources
    Establishing God's Kingdom
    Cities in the West

Cultures in Conflict
    Confronting the Plains Tribes
    The Fort Laramie Council, 1851
    Overwhelming the Mexican Settlers

Conclusion: Fruits of Manifest Destiny

(2) SIGNIFICANT THEMES AND HIGHLIGHTS

1. As the contrasting views of Narcissa Whitman and the Cayuse Indians make clear, the story of the trans-Mississippi West in the nineteenth century is not just the story of the acquisition of territory, but the experience of thousands of ordinary citizens who migrated to the frontier as well.

2. The chapter emphasizes the use of personal documents, especially the diaries written by men and women on the Overland Trail, in reconstructing historical realities.

3. The political and military events that led to the successful acquisition of western lands came at the expense of Native Americans and Mexicans. The events of this period are presented not only through the eyes of white emigrants but also from the perspective of these two groups.

4. Lewis Cass's attitudes and ideas exemplify the point of view and rhetoric of expansionists who advocated the acquisition of new territories.

(3) LEARNING GOALS

Familiarity with Basic Knowledge

After reading this chapter, you should be able to:

1. Define Manifest Destiny.

2. List the sequence of events resulting in the acquisition of Texas, New Mexico, California, and Oregon. Locate on a map and date the major territorial acquisitions of the United States between 1803 and 1853.

3. Describe the typical emigrant and three motives leading to the decision to migrate to the Far West.

4. List four ways in which white emigration affected the livelihood of Plains Indians.

5. Explain the terms of the Laramie Council agreements and assess their impact on red-white relations.

6. Contrast the experience of Mexican-Americans in Texas, New Mexico, and California.

Practice in Historical Thinking Skills

After reading this chapter, you should be able to:

1. Discuss the United States's policies toward the Plains Indians, placing those events in the context of Indian-white relations until the early 1850s.

2. Compare and contrast opportunities on the mining and farming frontiers.

3. Analyze the role of men and women on the Overland Trail.

(4) IMPORTANT DATES AND NAMES TO KNOW

1803-1806	Lewis and Clark expedition
1818	Treaty on joint U.S.-British occupation of Oregon
1819	Spain cedes Spanish territory in United States and sets transcontinental boundary of the Louisiana Purchase, excluding Texas
1821	Mexican independence Opening of Santa Fe Trail Stephen Austin leads American settlement of Texas
1821-1840	Native American removals
1830	Mexico abolishes slavery in Texas
1836	Battles of the Alamo and San Jacinto Texas declares independence
1840s	Emigrant crossings of overland trails.
1844	James Polk elected president
1845	"Manifest Destiny" coined United States annexes Texas and sends troops to the Rio Grande Americans attempt to buy Upper California and New Mexico
1846	Mexico declares defensive war United States declares war and takes Santa Fe Resolution of Oregon question
1847	Attack on Veracruz and Mexico City Mormon migration to Utah begins
1848	Treaty of Guadalupe Hidalgo

1849	California gold rush begins
1850	California admitted to the Union
1851	Fort Laramie Treaty
1853	Gadsden Purchase
1862	Homestead Act

Other Names to Know

Sam Houston	Antonio López de Santa Anna	Nicholas Trist
Zachary Taylor	John Slidell	Narcissa Whitman
Stephen W. Kearney	John L. O'Sullivan	

(5) GLOSSARY OF IMPORTANT TERMS

emigrant: term used to describe Americans moving to western frontiers

Manifest Destiny: the belief in the political, religious, and cultural superiority of American civilization, giving Americans an inherent right to the continent and "true title" to its lands

polygamy: a form of marriage in which a husband has more than one wife; believed by nineteenth-century Mormons to be divinely sanctioned

(6) ENRICHMENT IDEAS

1. The Recovering the Past section gives examples of diaries and personal documents written on the Overland Trail and suggests that men and women differed in the content and style of what they wrote in their diaries and journals. Many diaries have been collected and published. Read some of them. What seem to be the typical daily concerns of men? Of women? What can you conclude about the nature of trail life? What work was involved in moving west? What can you learn about family and social life through the diaries? Finally, do you find differences between journals written by men and those written by women? How do you connect these materials with the cult of domesticity and the idea of separate spheres for men and women?

2. The letters of many of the young men who participated in the gold rush are found in printed collections. Some may also be on file with your local historical society, as the men wrote letters to friends and family at home. What picture of mining life can you form from these personal documents? How much opportunity was there in the mining West as reflected in these letters? Did the writers have reasonable expectations of their future?

117

What can you tell about family life and the social character of mining life through reading the letters?

3. In some parts of the United States (Alaska, the West), a later frontier period is still fresh in the memories of older residents. This provides an excellent opportunity for an oral history.

4. On an outline map of the United States, draw in and date the major territorial acquisitions between 1803 and 1853 and the major overland trails and important junctions.

(7) SAMPLE TEST AND EXAMINATION QUESTIONS

Multiple choice: Choose the best answer.

1. Which of the following groups is not matched with the appropriate area?
   a. Five Civilized Tribes and the Oklahoma Territory.
   b. Settlers and squatters and Texas.
   c. Fur trappers and traders and the Rocky Mountain region.
   d. New England shippers and New Mexico.

2. The expression "Manifest Destiny" refers to
   a. the title of a journal published in the 1840s.
   b. a speech made by Lewis Cass.
   c. the Puritan belief of the uniqueness of the American experience.
   d. a belief that because of the superiority of its institutions, Americans should control the North American continent.

3. The Transcontinental Treaty of 1819
   a. clearly indicated that Texas belonged to the United States.
   b. excluded Texas as part of the United States.
   c. made clear that Texas had been part of the Louisiana Purchase.
   d. clearly included Oregon as belonging to the United States.

4. The Mexican government invited American settlers to Texas
   a. because they feared Texas was weak and needed settlers.
   b. because they wanted to gain converts for the Catholic church.
   c. because they hoped to see the introduction of American law in this area.
   d. because they wanted the labor of black slaves there.

5. Texas did not join the Union in 1837
   a. because Texans were still fighting the Mexicans for their independence.
   b. because Texans wished to have their own independent republic.
   c. because many northerners, fearful of the expansion of slavery, opposed annexation.
   d. because Jackson refused to take the advice of his "kitchen cabinet."

6. Polk's objectives in the conflict with Mexico included
   a. obtaining California.
   b. obtaining New Mexico.
   c. settling the boundary of Texas at the Rio Grande.
   d. all of the above.

7. The war with Mexico
   a. was complicated by the Oregon question.
   b. was clearly Mexico's fault.
   c. ended in 1848.
   d. was popular throughout the United States.

8. The acquisition of the Oregon country gave the United States land in the Northwest
   a. up to the line 54°40' north latitude.
   b. up to the 49th parallel.
   c. around San Francisco.
   d. all of the above.

9. Most overland emigrants traveled
   a. with strangers.
   b. with relatives and friends.
   c. with people of their own religion.
   d. alone.

10. The overland trip to Oregon
    a. was so expensive that only the rich could go west.
    b. was so cheap that virtually anyone could become an emigrant.
    c. cost a substantial amount, making the trip possible only for middle-class Americans.
    d. cost far more than making the trip by sea.

11. On the mining frontier
    a. most miners struck it rich.
    b. most people expected to make a fortune and build expensive houses in the West.
    c. miners who failed to get rich quick soon became wage earners.
    d. prostitutes were courteously treated because there were so few women.

12. In Utah
    a. most families were polygamous.
    b. Mormon men usually had more than two wives.
    c. polygamous wives frequently tried to escape.
    d. few families practiced polygamy.

13. The Native Americans of the Great Plains
    a. fiercely attacked the emigrants from the beginning.
    b. at first fought one another as much as they did white emigrants.
    c. provided buffalo barbecues for emigrants passing through their lands.
    d. saw no threat from white emigration.

14. All of the following are true about the Fort Laramie Council EXCEPT that it
    a. drew tribal boundaries.
    b. secured promises from some of those present to stay within tribal boundaries.
    c. succeeded in firmly establishing the reservation policy.
    d. gave Native Americans presents and other forms of compensation.

15. The Treaty of Guadalupe Hidalgo
    a. assured former Mexicans that they would enjoy the rights of citizens.
    b. promised the protection of their property.
    c. seemed to legitimate land grants made by Mexico.
    d. all of the above.

Identify and show a relationship between each of the following pairs:

mining frontier	*and*	bandidos
Fort Laramie Council	*and*	"fifty-four forty or fight"
Manifest Destiny	*and*	the Trail of Tears
Treaty of Guadalupe Hidalgo	*and*	Lewis Cass
Overland Trail	*and*	the Homestead Act

Essays

1. "Manifest Destiny was a policy for whites only." Discuss with specific evidence to support your main points.

2. Although the westward movement may not have realized dreams of opportunity, the fact of emigration did help keep American ideals alive. Write an essay either agreeing or disagreeing with the statement.

3. Analyze the myths and realities of popular images of the American West, specifically in regard to Native Americans and Hispanics.

4. Explain the role that religious attitudes had on the settlement of the West. In what specific cases was it strongest?

Map Question

Locate the following on the accompanying map.

1. The Trail of Tears
2. Oregon and California trails
3. Texas Republic, 1836–1845
4. Sioux and Cheyenne lands
5. Sutter's Fort, California
6. Mormon Trail's end, Salt Lake City
7. Rio Grande
8. Colorado River
9. Territory acquired under the
   Treaty of Guadalupe Hidalgo, 1848

10. Gadsden Purchase
11. Santa Fe Trail
12. Oregon country acquisition, 1846
13. San Francisco
14. Hopi and Navaho lands
15. Black belt
16. Erie Canal

14

The Union in Peril

(1) CHAPTER OUTLINE

As Abraham Lincoln awaits the election returns in November 1860, three other Americans—Robert Allston, a South Carolina slave owner; Frederick Douglass, an escaped slave; and Michael Luark, an Iowa farmer—also watch the results of the election, each filled with intense concern over how the fate of the nation would affect his own.

Slavery in the Territories
Free Soil or Constitutional Protection?
Popular Sovereignty and the Election of 1848
The Compromise of 1850
Consequences of Compromise

Political Disintegration
Weakened Party Politics in the Early 1850s
The Kansas-Nebraska Act
Expansionist "Young America" in the Larger World
Nativism, Know-Nothings, and Republicans

Kansas and the Two Cultures
Competing for Kansas
"Bleeding Kansas"
Northern Views and Visions
The Southern Perspective

Polarization and the Road to War
The *Dred Scott* Case
Constitutional Crisis in Kansas
Lincoln and the Illinois Debates
John Brown's Raid
The Election of 1860

The Divided House Falls
Secession and Uncertainty
Lincoln and Fort Sumter

Conclusion: The "Irrepressible Conflict"

(2) SIGNIFICANT THEMES AND HIGHLIGHTS

1. The heightened tensions surrounding the 1860 election and suggested by the anecdote indicate the central place the Civil War occupies in American history. The causes of the war that dissolved the Union, therefore, are crucial to an understanding of America's history. The causes reflect the interrelationship of politics, emotions, and sectional culture.

2. Historians have long debated, without resolution, the causes of the Civil War. This chapter focuses on four developments of the period between 1848 and 1861, each an important cause of war. The chapter weaves these developments together in an interpretive narrative account of both the events and the cultural values behind the events. The student is left to decide how the four causes interacted to bring about the war and which, if any, were more important than others.

3. Events in Kansas in 1855 and 1856 are highlighted as a specific microscopic illustration bringing together many of the forces that led Americans to secession and civil war in 1861.

4. The primary focus in this chapter is on national political developments involving nationally known figures because the Civil War was, after all, fundamentally a political event. Nevertheless, the chapter includes the comments of ordinary Americans, most frequently those of two figures from earlier chapters, runaway slave Frederick Douglass and South Carolina rice planter Robert Allston, as they observed the events of the 1850s leading to the outbreak of civil war.

(3) LEARNING GOALS

Familiarity with Basic Knowledge

After reading this chapter, you should be able to:

1. Explain four proposals for dealing with the territories acquired in the Mexican War and the four provisions of the Compromise of 1850.

2. Describe the breakdown of political parties in the early 1850s, explaining the disappearance of old parties and the emergence of new ones.

3. Outline the course of the Kansas-Nebraska Act and how it affected politics and sectional animosities in the mid-1850s.

4. Explain America's expansionist interest in Latin America.

5. Show how the events in Kansas in 1855 and 1856, the *Dred Scott* case, the emotional events of 1859–1860, and the election of Lincoln led to the secession crisis and the outbreak of the Civil War.

Practice in Historical Thinking Skills

After reading this chapter, you should be able to:

1. Describe the differing cultural values of the South and North and each section's view of the other, and explain how these cultural differences helped lead to civil war.

2. Explain the development and significance of each of the four causes of the Civil War, citing four or five specific examples for each.

3. Evaluate the four causes, indicating which ones (or one) you think were most significant in explaining why the North and South went to war in 1861.

(4) IMPORTANT DATES AND NAMES TO KNOW

1832	Nullification crisis
1835-1840	Intensification of abolitionist attacks on slavery Violent retaliatory attacks on abolitionists
1846	Wilmot Proviso
1848	Free-Soil party founded Zachary Taylor elected president
1850	Compromise of 1850, including Fugitive Slave Act
1850-1854	"Young America" movement
1851	Women's rights convention in Akron, Ohio
1852	Harriet Beecher Stowe publishes *Uncle Tom's Cabin* Franklin Pierce elected president
1854	Ostend Manifesto Kansas-Nebraska Act nullifies Missouri Compromise Republican and Know-Nothing parties formed
1855	Walt Whitman publishes *Leaves of Grass*

1855-1856	Thousands pour into Kansas, creating months of turmoil and violence
1856	John Brown's massacre in Kansas Sumner-Brooks incident in Senate James Buchanan elected president
1857	*Dred Scott* decision legalizes slavery in territories Lecompton constitution in Kansas
1858	Lincoln-Douglas debates
1859	John Brown's raid at Harpers Ferry
1860	Democratic party splits Four-party campaign Abraham Lincoln elected president
1860-1861	Seven southern states secede
1861	Confederate States of America founded Attack on Fort Sumter begins Civil War

Other Names to Know

Lewis Cass	Orestes Brownson	William Marcy
William Walker	Frederick Douglass	William Seward
Henry Clay	John C. Frémont	Millard Fillmore
David Atchison	Roger Taney	John C. Breckinridge
Major Robert Anderson	General P. G. T. Beauregard	

(5) GLOSSARY OF IMPORTANT TERMS

nativism: antiforeign feelings and behavior (especially against Irish Catholic immigrants) expressed by native-born Americans

popular sovereignty: the doctrine that left the decision whether a state would enter the Union slave or free up to the territorial legislature representing the people of that territory

Young America: a term describing proud, confident, highly nationalistic, expansionist Americans in the early 1850s

(6) ENRICHMENT IDEAS

1. After reviewing the Recovering the Past section, read further into the Senate debates over the Compromise of 1850, analyzing and discussing the style and arguments of various speeches, especially the complete texts of those by Clay, Webster, Calhoun, and Seward.

2. It is 1855. Create a dialogue between two recent migrants to Kansas, one from Massachusetts and one from Missouri. Put them in an appropriate setting and provide an end to their conversation, but focus mainly on how each reveals his or her sectional origins and views and how each sees the other.

3. You are Lincoln in the winter of 1860–1861. What would you do? You are Frederick Douglass in the same winter. What would you do? You are Robert Allston at the same time. What would you do? Why? What do you think would happen?

(7) SAMPLE TEST AND EXAMINATION QUESTIONS

Multiple choice: Choose the best answer.

1. According to the textbook, the most pervasive underlying cause of the Civil War was
   a. slavery.
   b. political blundering.
   c. abolitionist agitation.
   d. economic differences.

2. The Wilmot Proviso stated that
   a. Congress should protect slavery in the territories acquired from Mexico.
   b. the people of those territories should decide for themselves whether to permit slavery.
   c. slavery should be prohibited in territories acquired from Mexico.
   d. slavery should be prohibited only north of the line 36°30'.

3. The Compromise of 1850 included all of the following provisions EXCEPT
   a. a stronger Fugitive Slave Act.
   b. the admission of California as a free state.
   c. the abolition of slavery and the slave trade in the District of Columbia.
   d. the organization of New Mexico and Utah according to the principle of popular sovereignty.

4. Of those blacks arrested in the North under the Fugitive Slave Act, most
   a. were able to purchase their freedom.
   b. were returned to the South.
   c. escaped and fled to Canada.
   d. were rescued by sympathetic whites.

5. Central to the nativist fears was
   a. the growing power of slaveholders.
   b. a dislike of anyone who favored abolitionism.
   c. a hatred of the wealthy.
   d. loathing of the Roman Catholic church.

6. Party distinctiveness and loyalty decreased in the early 1850s because of
   a. improving economic conditions.
   b. the upsurge of expansionist fervor.
   c. Fillmore's friendship with Douglas.
   d. the lasting success of the Compromise of 1850.

7. The Kansas-Nebraska Act
   a. settled the question of slavery in the territories.
   b. unified the Democratic party.
   c. guaranteed Douglas the presidential nomination in 1856.
   d. seriously weakened Douglas's support from northern Democrats.

8. The Know-Nothing party advocated
   a. a lengthy period before immigrants could become citizens.
   b. the abolition of slavery.
   c. government regulation of Catholic parochial schools.
   d. all of the above.

9. The Republican party in 1860
   a. stood for the principle of popular sovereignty.
   b. opposed the extension of slavery into the territories.
   c. advocated the abolition of slavery.
   d. promised not to interfere with southern slavery but supported equal rights for free blacks in the North.

10. Which of the following is in the correct chronological order?
    a. Kansas-Nebraska Act, Fugitive Slave Act, Dred Scott case.
    b. Fugitive Slave Act, Kansas-Nebraska Act, Dred Scott case.
    c. Fugitive Slave Act, Dred Scott case, Kansas-Nebraska Act.
    d. Dred Scott case, Kansas-Nebraska Act, Fugitive Slave Act.

11. The Ostend Manifesto claimed Cuba as a natural part of the United States because of
    a. geographic proximity and mutual economic interests.
    b. historic ties and treaty obligation.
    c. the influence of the United Fruit Company.
    d. all of the above.

12. Which of the following statements of the southern perspective is not true?
    a. Northerners were ill-mannered, mean, and materialistic.
    b. The South was a genteel and orderly society guided by gentleman planters.
    c. Slavery was an unfortunate but necessary evil resulting from high northern tariffs.
    d. Southerners revered local self-government as a basic republican right.

13. According to the Dred Scott decision,
    a. the Compromise of 1850 was declared unconstitutional.
    b. free blacks but not slaves had the right to sue in federal courts.
    c. Dred Scott was entitled to his freedom because he had lived in a free state.
    d. Dred Scott had no right to sue and was denied his freedom.

14. Of the options facing him in the winter of 1860–1861, Lincoln favored
    a. compromising with the secessionist states.
    b. letting secessionist states "go in peace."
    c. risking war by upholding the laws of the land and protecting federal property.
    d. going to war in a daring first strike against the secessionist states.

15. Which of the following is in the correct chronological order?
    a. John Brown's raid, secession of South Carolina, Lincoln's election, Fort Sumter.
    b. Lincoln's election, secession of South Carolina, John Brown's raid, Fort Sumter.
    c. John Brown's raid, Lincoln's election, secession of South Carolina, Fort Sumter.
    d. Lincoln's election, John Brown's raid, secession of South Carolina, Fort Sumter.

Essays

1. Explain your view of the causes of the Civil War, citing appropriate specific evidence to defend your explanation.

2. Select three or four specific events and developments in the 1850s that you think were the most significant in causing the Civil War. Defend your choices and explain why you think other events and developments were less significant.

3. Construct a dialogue between a New England migrant and a Missouri slaveholder over whether Kansas should become a slave or free state. Use your imagination in setting the scene (and the outcome), but focus your primary attention on how each person reflects his or her sectional view and how that section viewed the other.

4. Explain the reasons the majority on the Supreme Court used in deciding the *Dred Scott* v. *Sandford* case.

5. Explain why the Lincoln-Douglas debates in Illinois were significant to the outcome of the election of 1860.

Identify and Interpret: Cartoon
(that is, state who, what, where, when, and why significant)

129

15

The Union Severed

(1) CHAPTER OUTLINE

A young northern man, Arthur Carpenter, begs his parents for permission to join the army and wins their consent. A southern Presbyterian preacher, George Eagleton of Tennessee, feels compelled to enlist and leaves his sorrowful wife, Ethie, and their baby to go to war.

Organizing for War
> The Balance of Resources
> The Border States
> Challenges of War
> Lincoln and Davis

Clashing on the Battlefield, 1861–1862
> War in the East
> War in the West
> Naval Warfare
> Cotton Diplomacy
> Common Problems, Novel Solutions
> Political Dissension, 1862

The Tide Turns, 1863–1865
> The Emancipation Proclamation, 1863
> Unanticipated Consequences of War
> Changing Military Strategies, 1863–1865

Changes Wrought by War
> A New South
> The North
> On the Home Front, 1861–1865
> Wartime Race Relations
> Women and the War
> The Election of 1864
> Why the North Won
> The Costs of War
> Unanswered Questions

Conclusion: An Uncertain Future

(2) SIGNIFICANT THEMES AND HIGHLIGHTS

1. This chapter attempts to provide a coherent picture of the Civil War as a military and diplomatic event. But, as the stories of Arthur Carpenter and the Eagletons suggest, the chapter emphasizes the impact of the war on the lives of ordinary people: soldiers who fought the war and noncombatants behind the lines, such as women like Ethie Eagleton and Emily Harris, slaves, and working-class Americans.

2. In numerous, unanticipated ways, the war transformed northern and southern society. The changes were most dramatic in the South, where by the war's end leaders were contemplating the use of slaves as soldiers, and even emancipation. Ironically, although the war was fought to save distinctly different ways of life, the conflict forced both sides to adopt similar measures and to become more alike.

3. In the North, the war was fought to save the Union. Only gradually did goals shift to include the emancipation of slaves. Lincoln's racial leadership is emphasized despite his inability to reduce racism significantly in northern society.

4. The chapter continually shows the contrasts between northern and southern resources, leadership, military strategy, wartime political and economic problems and solutions, and the impact of the war on race relations, women, daily life, and other features of the home front.

(3) LEARNING GOALS

Familiarity with Basic Knowledge

After reading this chapter, you should be able to:

1. Compare and contrast the balance of resources in the North and the South at the war's beginning and its end.

2. State the significance of the border states to both the Union and the Confederacy.

3. Explain the basic military strategies of each side.

4. List the various manpower and financial measures taken by the Confederate and Union governments during the course of the war.

5. Describe the origins, purposes, and provisions of the Emancipation Proclamation.

6. List the ways in which Lincoln and Davis expanded presidential powers.

7. Describe the participation of women and African-Americans in the war.

Practice in Historical Thinking Skills

After reading this chapter, you should be able to:

1. Discuss the social, political, and economic impact of the war on both northern and southern societies and show how the South became increasingly similar to the North.

2. Analyze the impact of the Emancipation Proclamation on the course of the war and on race relations.

3. Analyze why the North won the war and the South lost it.

(4) IMPORTANT DATES AND NAMES TO KNOW

1861	Lincoln calls up state militia and suspends habeas corpus First Battle of Bull Run Union blockades the South
1862	Battles at Shiloh, Bull Run, and Antietam *Monitor* and *Virginia* battle First black regiment authorized by Union Union issues greenbacks South institutes military draft Pacific Railroad Act Homestead Act Morrill Land-Grant College Act
1863	Lincoln issues Emancipation Proclamation Congress adopts military draft Battles of Gettysburg and Vicksburg Union Banking Act Southern tax laws and impressment act New York draft riots Southern food riots
1864	Sherman's march through Georgia Lincoln re-elected Union Banking Act
1865	Lee surrenders at Appomattox Lincoln assassinated; Andrew Johnson becomes president

Other Names to Know

General Robert E. Lee	Roger Taney	Clara Barton
General Ulysses S. Grant	Jefferson Davis	Salmon Chase
General George McClellan	General William T. Sherman	Horace Greeley
General George Meade	Mathew Brady	

(5) GLOSSARY OF IMPORTANT TERMS

Anaconda Plan: Union strategy to blockade South on both land and sea

bounty: the fee, ranging from $800 and $1,000, paid to individuals by northern communities who wished to fill their military quota outside of their own communities

Confederacy: the name given to the new southern nation between 1861 and 1865

Copperheads: Northern Democrats who wished for a peaceful and speedy end to the war. The Republican press struck them with the label of the deadly snakes.

cotton diplomacy: the belief in the South that cotton would generate support for the Confederate cause in Europe

impressment: the confiscation or taking of private property for the war effort

radical: group of Republicans, never very many, who wished not only for the emancipation of the slaves but also for fundamental changes in southern society after the war

(6) ENRICHMENT IDEAS

1. Study a volume of photographs of the Civil War taken by Mathew Brady and others. Choose two or three photographs and study them closely. First, describe what they contain: What objects are in each? What people? How are they dressed? What are their expressions (faces and bodies)? What appears to be the relation between them? Then draw some conclusions: What atmosphere has been created? Why were the photos taken and for whom? What can you learn about the Civil War by studying photos of the conflict? What are the limitations of this kind of historical evidence? How has the technological level of the equipment shaped photography?

2. Study letters or diaries written by a participant in the Civil War. You may have some in your family, or check your college or university library archives; most historical societies will have manuscript resources of this kind. There are good printed collections of letters and diaries written by soldiers. You might also want to look at materials written by people at home. What kinds of experience does your writer describe? What seems important to him or her? What understanding of the war does your writer have?

3. If a Civil War battlefield is nearby, visit it. Imagine yourself a typical soldier writing home with news of that battle. What would you say?

(7) SAMPLE TEST AND EXAMINATION QUESTIONS

Multiple choice: Choose the best answer.

1. Early opponents of the war included all of the following EXCEPT
    a. free blacks in the North.
    b. white yeoman farmers who owned no slaves.
    c. Irish immigrants.
    d. northern Democrats from the Midwest.

2. In 1861, Lincoln planned to increase the army by
    a. calling up state militias for three months.
    b. dramatically increasing its size through bounties.
    c. immediately using the draft.
    d. using slaves who were offered freedom.

3. In 1861, the South had the advantage of
    a. a slave population that could be recruited for the army.
    b. substantial agricultural resources.
    c. a larger population of males than the North.
    d. an adequate railroad system.

4. All of the following border states eventually joined the Confederacy EXCEPT
    a. Virginia.
    b. Tennessee.
    c. Kentucky.
    d. Arkansas.

5. In the early days of the war, Lincoln
    a. scrupulously respected individual civil rights.
    b. revoked General Frémont's emancipation proclamation in Missouri.
    c. ordered the immediate recruitment of black soldiers.
    d. decided against a naval blockade of the South.

6. The first battle of Bull Run indicated
    a. that the southern army was on the way to becoming a professional fighting force.
    b. that northern commanders had a well-developed strategic plan to defeat the South.
    c. that a volunteer army would be sufficient for the conflict.
    d. the deficiencies of short-term enlistment.

7. Cotton diplomacy failed because
   a. European powers believed the South could not win the war.
   b. Europe was in a depression and could not buy cotton.
   c. European industrialists found other sources of cotton.
   d. European nations were not interested in the conflict.

8. The war was financed on both sides mostly by
   a. government borrowing.
   b. taxation.
   c. foreign loans.
   d. printing paper money.

9. In the South,
   a. all soldiers were drafted.
   b. about a third of the Confederate army was conscripted.
   c. many slaves served as soldiers.
   d. only slave owners served in the army.

10. In the North, moderate and conservative Republicans
    a. favored the emancipation of slaves.
    b. supported the use of blacks as soldiers.
    c. hoped for sweeping social and economic changes in the South.
    d. feared all of the above.

11. When it was issued, the Emancipation Proclamation technically freed
    a. slaves in the border states.
    b. free blacks only.
    c. slaves in areas conquered by Union armies.
    d. slaves in unconquered parts of the Confederacy.

12. The Confederate government
    a. honored the concept of states' rights.
    b. honored the principle of private property.
    c. favored conscription and taxation.
    d. favored using emancipated slaves as soldiers.

13. The demands of war produced
    a. deflation.
    b. inflation.
    c. increases in real wages.
    d. heavy unemployment.

14. Grant's final campaign
    a. was intended to secure the Mississippi River.
    b. was aimed at luring Lee into one final, decisive battle.
    c. was aimed at the total destruction of all Confederate armies and resources.
    d. depended on guerrilla warfare.

15. The Civil War
    a. was a tremendous boon to northern industry.
    b. stimulated northern manufacturing only in certain war-related industries.
    c. had surprisingly little effect on industry.
    d. created financial chaos and thus disrupted industry.

Identify and show a relationship between each of the following pairs:

Emily Harris	*and*	Arthur Carpenter
Emancipation Proclamation	*and*	Antietam
Jefferson Davis	*and*	Greenbacks
General William Sherman	*and*	"total war"
Vicksburg	*and*	Gettysburg

Essays

1. Think about and write essays on items 1–3 found in "Learning Goals" in the section "Practice in Historical Thinking Skills."

2. "If one is to understand the Civil War, it is important to realize that it was not fought to end slavery." Develop an essay showing the extent to which you agree or disagree with this statement.

3. "Lincoln's masterful leadership was the main ingredient of northern victory." To what extent do you agree or disagree with this statement?

Identify and Interpret: Quotation
(that is, state who, what, where, when, and why significant)

With malice toward none; with charity for all; with firmness in the right, as God gives us to see the right, let us strive on to finish the work we are in; to bind up the nation's wounds; to care for him who shall have borne the battle, and for his widow, and his orphan—to do all which may achieve and cherish a just, and a lasting peace, among ourselves, and with all nations.

Map Question

Locate the following on the accompanying map.

1. Washington, D.C.
2. The eleven Confederate States of America
3. Fort Sumter
4. Antietam and Bull Run
5. Shiloh
6. Vicksburg and Mississippi River
7. Gettysburg
8. Sherman's route to the sea
9. Montgomery, Alabama
10. The four border states remaining in the Union
11. Appomattox
12. New state seceding from Virginia, 1863

16

The Union Reconstructed

(1) CHAPTER OUTLINE

Adele and Elizabeth Allston fearfully return to their plantations after the war. At Nightingale Hall, they have a joyous reunion with their former slaves. But at Guendalos, the blacks are defiant, the atmosphere threatening. The morning after the arrival, however, Uncle Jacob, the former black driver, hands the keys to the crop barns over to the women, in recognition that they still own the land.

The Bittersweet Aftermath of War
> The United States in 1865
> Hopes Among the Freedpeople
> The White South's Fearful Response

National Reconstruction Politics
> Presidential Reconstruction by Proclamation
> Congressional Reconstruction by Amendment
> The President Impeached
> What Congressional Moderation Meant for Rebels, Blacks, and Women

The Lives of Freedpeople
> The Freedmen's Bureau
> Economic Freedom by Degrees
> White Farmers During Reconstruction
> Black Self-Help Institutions

Reconstruction in the Southern States
> Republican Rule
> Violence and "Redemption"
> Shifting National Priorities
> The End of Reconstruction

Conclusion: A Mixed Legacy

(2) SIGNIFICANT THEMES AND HIGHLIGHTS

1. The account of the Allstons' return to their plantations highlights the focus of this chapter. The primary action of the chapter takes place on the old southern plantation and in the former slave's cabins, not in the halls of Congress and the White House. Rather than emphasizing the political programs and conflicts of Congress and the president, we see the hopes and fears of ordinary persons—both black and white—as they faced their postwar world. Political events in the North as well as in the South in the years between 1865 and 1877 are included, but they are secondary to the psychosocial dynamics of reconstructing new relationships among differing people after the Civil War.

2. As reflected in the opening anecdote, the dreams and aspirations of three groups—white southerners, former slaves, and white northerners—are introduced and woven together throughout the chapter. The main question of the chapter is: What happens as these three sets of goals come into conflict? Uncle Jacob's return of the keys to the crop barns to the Allston family, a gesture symbolic of ownership, indicates the crucial importance of labor and land to an understanding of the outcome of these conflicting goals. The result was a mixed legacy of human gains and losses.

3. The experiences of the Allston family are concluded in this chapter. Frederick Douglass's astute observations as a black leader continue as those of W. E. B. Du Bois begin.

4. The tragic elements of the Reconstruction, or any other era, are perhaps best represented in literature. Novels and short stories are used in this chapter to capture these human conflicts.

(3) LEARNING GOALS

Familiarity with Basic Knowledge

After reading this chapter, you should be able to:

1. State four or five particular goals of three groups—the freedpeople, white southerners, and white northerners—at the end of the Civil War.

2. Describe the situation and mood of the country at the end of the Civil War and describe the first programs and actions of southern whites and former slaves as they redefined race relations in 1865.

3. Explain President Johnson's reconstruction program and contrast it with Congress's alternative program.

4. Name and explain three important acts and three constitutional amendments that were part of the Republican Reconstruction program.

5. Explain the arrangements for working the land that developed between white landowners and the former slaves and describe the terms of a typical work contract.

6. Describe the character of the Republican state governments in the South during Reconstruction: Who ruled? How well? For how long? How did these governments come to an end?

7. Explain how Reconstruction ended.

Practice in Historical Thinking Skills

After reading this chapter, you should be able to:

1. Assess the relationship between the character of national politics during Grant's term of office from 1869 to 1877 and the end of Reconstruction in the South.

2. Show how the diverse goals of the white southerners, former slaves, and white northerners came into conflict, and assess to what extent each group achieved its various goals by the end of Reconstruction.

3. Evaluate the respective roles southern and northern whites played in impeding black goals.

(4) IMPORTANT DATES AND NAMES TO KNOW

1865	Civil War ends
	Lincoln assassinated; Andrew Johnson becomes president
	Johnson proposes general amnesty and reconstruction plan
	Racial confusion, widespread hunger, and demobilization
	Thirteenth Amendment ratified (abolishing slavery)
	Freedmen's Bureau established
1865-1866	Black codes
	Repossession of land by whites and freedpeople's contracts
1866	Freedmen's Bureau renewed and Civil Rights Act passed over Johnson's veto
	Southern Homestead Act
	Ku Klux Klan formed
1867	Reconstruction Acts passed over Johnson's veto
	Impeachment controversy
	Freedmen's Bureau ends
1868	Fourteenth Amendment ratified
	Senate fails to convict Johnson of Impeachment charges
	Ulysses S. Grant elected president
1868-1870	Ten states readmitted under congressional plan

1869	Georgia and Virginia reestablish Democratic party control
1870	Fifteenth Amendment ratified
1870s-1880s	Black "exodusters" migrate to Kansas
1870-1871	Force Acts North Carolina and Georgia reestablish Democratic party control
1872	Grant re-elected president
1873	Crédit Mobilier scandal Panic causes depression
1874	Alabama and Arkansas reestablish Democratic party control
1875	Civil Rights Act passed Mississippi reestablishes Democratic party control
1876	Hayes-Tilden election
1876-1877	South Carolina, Louisiana, and Florida reestablish Democratic party control
1877	Compromise of 1877 Rutherford B. Hayes assumes presidency and ends Reconstruction
1880s	Tenancy and sharecropping prevail in the South Disfranchisement and segregation of southern blacks begins

Other Names to Know

Edwin Stanton	Jay Gould	General O. O. Howard
Susan B. Anthony	Charles Sumner	Thaddeus Stevens
Frederick Douglass	Benjamin "Pap" Singleton	Elizabeth Cady Stanton
W. E. B. Du Bois		

(5) GLOSSARY OF IMPORTANT TERMS

amnesty: removing blame and punishment for past crimes

carpetbagger: a derogatory term applied to northerners who settled in the South after the Civil War

debt slavery/peonage: the economic situation in which tenant farmers or sharecroppers become trapped in perpetual debt because they always owe more to their landlords than they get from the sale of cotton or other crops

exodusters: disillusioned blacks who fled the South in the 1870s and 1880s to settle in all-black towns in the western prairies

freedmen: former slaves emancipated by the Thirteenth Amendment

Grantism: a term describing political corruption and graft in the North in the 1870s

radical Republicans: a derogatory term applied to northern Republican politicians who generally wanted not only to punish the ex-Confederate leaders but also to help the former slaves fulfill their goals (overstated term; most Republicans were moderate)

redemption: a word used by southerners to describe the return of conservative Democrats to power in southern state governments, thus removing the so-called radical Republicans from power

scalawag: a derogatory term applied to southern Unionists who supported Republican state governments during Reconstruction

"waving the bloody shirt": a Republican political campaign tactic of reminding voters of the Civil War and the valuable role of the Republican party in preserving the Union and defeating the rebellious (Democratic) South

(6) ENRICHMENT IDEAS

1. The "Recovering the Past" section, which focuses on the ways in which novels reflect history, includes only a very brief excerpt from two novels about Reconstruction. Consider, in a longer excerpt, the style and point of view of the authors of the six novels listed below. Which do you think most accurately reflects the historical truth about Reconstruction? Is the most accurate novel-as-history necessarily the best as literature? Based on these excerpts, which novel do you think you would like to read in its entirety and why?

   Thomas Dixon, Jr., *The Clansman*
   Albion Tourgée, *A Fool's Errand*
   Howard Fast, *Freedom Road*
   W. E. B. Du Bois, *Quest of the Silver Fleece*
   John DeForest, *Miss Ravenal's Conversion from Secession to Loyalty*
   Earnest Gaines, *The Autobiography of Miss Jane Pittman*

2. Complete the textbook chart "Conflicting Goals During Reconstruction" for the following groups in 1865 by showing what happened to each group by 1877. How well were each of their earlier goals fulfilled? When you have completed the chart, you are in a position to assess the success of Reconstruction and to understand developments in the South into the twentieth century.

   a. victorious northern "radical" Republicans
   b. northern moderates—Republicans and Democrats
   c. old southern planter aristocracy (former Confederates)
   d. new "Other South": yeoman farmers and former Whigs (unionists)
   e. black freedpeople

3. Write a short story, or a series of letters or diary entries, describing the typical daily experiences of various persons during Reconstruction. For example, a southern woman, Adele Allston, or her daughter Elizabeth, presiding over a large cotton plantation in the absence of their husband and father, who was killed in the war. Or a black family that had been given 40 acres of confiscated land by a northern general during the war and faced a title dispute with, and dispossession by, the original landowner afterwards. Or a poor white family putting its life together in the changing economic climate and race relationships of the postwar years. Or a Yankee schoolteacher's experiences in a Freedmen's Bureau school in Tennessee. Or a Freedmen's Bureau agent's hectic, overworked, and underappreciated daily duties in Mississippi. Read in class and discuss. Notice the clash of unresolved dreams.

(7) SAMPLE TEST AND EXAMINATION QUESTIONS

Multiple choice: Choose the best answer.

1. Which of the following is in the correct order?
    a. Black codes, Fourteenth Amendment, Mississippi Plan.
    b. Fourteenth Amendment, Mississippi Plan, Reconstruction Acts.
    c. Black codes, Mississippi Plan, Fourteenth Amendment.
    d. Mississippi Plan, Black codes, Reconstruction Acts.

2. All of the following are true descriptions of the United States in spring 1865 EXCEPT
    a. many southern cities were physically devastated.
    b. black ex-slaves were in a confused state of semi-freedom.
    c. former Confederates wanted to restore as much of the old social order as possible.
    d. most northerners wanted to severely punish southern rebels physically and economically.

3. Which one is NOT true of the ex-slaves in the first months of emancipation?
    a. They went searching for missing family members.
    b. They selected surnames.
    c. They showed great interest in getting an education.
    d. They left their masters as soon as possible, usually stealing property as an expression of revenge.

4. Congressional Republicans passed all of the following bills EXCEPT
   a. a land bill granting 40 acres and a mule to black Union veterans.
   b. a civil rights bill.
   c. Reconstruction acts dividing the South into five military districts.
   d. a bill extending the Freedmen's Bureau.

5. The heart of President Johnson's Reconstruction program was
   a. to punish all wealthy ex-Confederates by confiscating their land.
   b. general amnesty and pardons for most ex-Confederates.
   c. insistence on passage of the Fourteenth Amendment.
   d. a land bill for poor and middle-class southern whites.

6. The most obvious failure of the Freedmen's Bureau was in its role of
   a. distributing emergency rations.
   b. setting the freed slaves up on their own land.
   c. setting up schools for the freed slaves.
   d. facilitating family reunions and marriage and work for the freed slaves.

7. Most Republican politicians in the Reconstruction era were motivated by all of the following EXCEPT
   a. the desire to maintain political power.
   b. some idealistic concern for protecting the civil rights of the freed slaves.
   c. a vindictive desire to confiscate rebel land and redistribute it among blacks.
   d. a concern for securing the continued economic growth of northern industry.

8. Republican state governments in the South were
   a. dominated by blacks.
   b. dominated by "carpetbaggers" and "scalawags."
   c. effective at eliminating undemocratic features of the pre-war governments.
   d. the most corrupt in the nation.

9. State governments in the South during Reconstruction accomplished all of the following EXCEPT
   a. providing public school systems.
   b. approving generous measures for economic rebuilding.
   c. liberalizing divorce and penal laws.
   d. guaranteeing universal male suffrage.

10. The Democrats returned to power in the South because
    a. the Republicans made such a mess of the tax system.
    b. blacks became Democrats when they did not receive 40 acres and a mule.
    c. secret organizations used violence to drive out Republicans.
    d. Grant realized that the Republican party was harming itself by its policies on the state level.

11. By the 1870s, the Republican party
    a. was reinforced as the party of moral reform and black rights.
    b. became more and more a party representing big business.
    c. blocked most transportation schemes.
    d. supported women's rights.

12. Grant's administration was characterized by
    a. scandals like the Whiskey Ring affair.
    b. an excess of democracy.
    c. zealous attempts to reduce graft.
    d. none of the above.

13. The Civil Rights Act of 1875
    a. condemned the Ku Klux Klan for violations of the Fourteenth Amendment.
    b. passed the House but was defeated in the Senate.
    c. passed both houses of Congress but was vetoed by the president.
    d. was passed by Congress and signed by the president but not really enforced.

14. The significance of the election of 1877 was that it
    a. ended Reconstruction.
    b. resulted in the removal of the last federal troops from the South.
    c. resulted in federal aid for the South.
    d. all of the above.

15. Which best summarizes the nation in 1877?
    a. Reconstruction had fulfilled the dreams of the freedmen.
    b. The white South had won everything during Reconstruction that they had lost during the war.
    c. Concern for rights and condition of the freedmen was no longer a major priority.
    d. Women were the real winners of Reconstruction because they could now vote.

Briefly identify and show a relationship between each of the following pairs.

General O. O. Howard	*and*	Thaddeus Stevens
Black codes	*and*	the Fourteenth Amendment
proclamation of general amnesty	*and*	the Reconstruction Acts
freedmen work contracts	*and*	southern homestead acts
Mississippi Plan of 1875	*and*	Force Act of 1870-1871
"40 acres and a mule"	*and*	"peace at any price"
annual wage contract	*and*	sharecropping

Essays

1. Use items 1-3 under "Practice in Historical Thinking Skills" in the "Learning Goals" section to develop essays.

2. In *The Souls of Black Folk,* W. E. B. DuBois wrote: "So the Freedmen's Bureau died, and its child was the Fifteenth Amendment." Discuss, showing how this statement might be interpreted as an apt summary of Reconstruction.

3. In *The Souls of Black Folk*, W. E. B. DuBois says: "Negro suffrage ended a civil war by beginning a race feud." Discuss the heritage of Reconstruction. To what extent did the events of that period create a continuing race feud in America, sectional animosity, and patterns of political party allegiance? To what extent do these phenomena still exist? How would you have done better?

ANSWERS TO SAMPLE TEST AND EXAMINATION QUESTIONS*

Chapter 1	Chapter 2	Chapter 3	Chapter 4	Chapter 5
1. a	1. c	1. c	1. a	1. c
2. d	2. b	2. b	2. d	2. a
3. b	3. a	3. a	3. c	3. d
4. b	4. a	4. a	4. d	4. a
5. d	5. b	5. d	5. d	5. b
6. c	6. c	6. a	6. c	6. c
7. d	7. b	7. b	7. c	7. c
8. c	8. d	8. b	8. c	8. b
9. c	9. a	9. a	9. d	9. c
10. a	10. d	10. c	10. a	10. b
11. c	11. c	11. c	11. b	11. d
12. c	12. c	12. c	12. c	12. c
13. c	13. a	13. d	13. d	13. b
14. d	14. d	14. c	14. b	14. d
15. b	15. c	15. a	15. d	15. a
			16. a	

Chapter 6

Multiple Choice	Order & Dates
1. a	1. 1763 End of Seven Years' War
2. b	2. 1765 Stamp Act
3. b	3. 1770 "Boston Massacre"
4. a	4. 1773 Boston Tea Party
5. c	5. 1775 Lexington and Concord
6. d	6. 1776 Declaration of Independence
7. c	7. 1777 Battle of Saratoga
8. a	8. 1778 French treaty of alliance and commerce
9. b	9. 1781 Yorktown
10. b	10. 1783 Treaty of Paris
11. d	
12. c	
13. d	
14. c	

Answers to the Quotation and Chart Identifications and the Map Questions are found at the end of this section.

Chapter 7		Chapter 8	Chapter 9
Multiple Choice	True/False		
1. a	1. True	1. c	1. c
2. b	2. False	2. b	2. c
3. d	3. True	3. b	3. b
4. d	4. True	4. c	4. a
5. a	5. False	5. a	5. b
6. c	6. True	6. c	6. d
7. d	7. False	7. d	7. a
8. c	8. True	8. a	8. b
9. a	9. False	9. b	9. c
10. c	10. True	10. d	10. b
11. d	11. True	11. a	11. b
12. a	12. True	12. b	12. a
13. b	13. False	13. c	13. d
	14. False	14. b	14. a
	15. False		15. d
	16. True		
	17. False		
	18. False		

Chapter 10	Chapter 11	Chapter 12	
		Multiple Choice	Matching
1. d	1. c	1. c	1. e
2. b	2. d	2. b	2. l
3. b	3. a	3. d	3. a
4. c	4. a	4. b	4. f
5. d	5. b	5. b	5. j
6. b	6. a	6. c	6. i
7. d	7. a	7. b	7. n
8. a	8. c	8. c	8. c
9. c	9. b	9. b	9. m
10. c	10. c	10. b	10. o
11. b	11. c	11. a	11. b
12. d	12. b	12. d	12. h
13. c	13. b	13. b	13. d
14. c	14. b	14. d	14. k
15. b	15. c	15. b	15. g
16. a	16. c		
17. c			

Chapter 13	Chapter 14	Chapter 15	Chapter 16
		Multiple Choice	
1. d	1. a	1. a	1. a
2. d	2. c	2. a	2. d
3. b	3. c	3. b	3. d
4. a	4. b	4. c	4. a
5. c	5. d	5. b	5. b
6. d	6. a	6. d	6. b
7. c	7. d	7. c	7. c
8. b	8. a	8. d	8. c
9. b	9. b	9. b	9. d
10. c	10. b	10. d	10. c
11. c	11. a	11. d	11. b
12. d	12. c	12. c	12. a
13. b	13. d	13. b	13. d
14. c	14. c	14. c	14. d
15. d	15. c	15. b	15. c

ANSWERS: IDENTIFY AND INTERPRET

Chapter 3 – Quotation

John Winthrop, "A Model of Christian Charity," a sermon delivered on board the *Arbella* while crossing the Atlantic in 1630. A statement of the importance of a covenant, both among the Puritans and with God, in establishing a model community of saints for others to admire and imitate.

Chapter 4 – Quotation

Jonathan Edwards, "Sinners in the Hand of an Angry God," Enfield, Connecticut, 1741. One of the most famous and powerful sermons during the Great Awakening.

Chapter 6 – Quotation

Abigail Adams, letter to husband John Adams, 1776, as he is preparing to sign the Declaration of Independence. An early feminist reminder that revolutionary "natural" rights in America were for white men only and that women would use familiar arguments in achieving their liberation.

Chapter 7 – Quotation

Anti-Federalist (Patrick Henry) argument against ratification of the Constitution, Virginia, 1788. In a debate with James Madison, Henry states the classic case that the states, not the people, formed the compact creating the new government. The argument would be reiterated until the Civil War settled the issues.

Chapter 8 – Quotation

Thomas Jefferson, Inaugural Address, 1801. Although seeking reconciliation with the Federalists, Jefferson articulates the Republican program of expansion ("with room enough. . .," limited government, equality of opportunity, and religious and economic freedom.

Chapter 10 – Quotation

Regulations from a New England boarding house for women workers in the mills, from the 1820s or 1830s. The rules were an attempt to ensure that women workers lived in a respectable manner and had enough sleep to work efficiently. The regulations highlight the regimentation of life in a mill town but also hint at the sense of sisterhood which these boarding house arrangements often fostered.

Chapter 12 – Quotation

Declaration of Sentiments, Women's Rights Convention, Seneca Falls, New York, 1848. Drafted by Elizabeth Cady Stanton, and modeled on the Declaration of Independence, the Seneca Falls Declaration and resolutions signaled the women's rights agenda for the century to follow.

Chapter 12 – Chart: Public Land Sales, 1820–1860

1. The chart illustrates the pattern of public land sales between 1820 and 1860. The decades of the 1830s and the 1850s saw spectacular increases in the sale of public lands, followed by sharp declines. Note the Panic of 1837 and subsequent depression.

2. Some of the factors which contributed to the patterns apparent here include the opening of new territories for settlement, legislation which made it easier and cheaper for Americans to acquire land, improvements in transportation and the growth of markets which made settlement attractive, land hunger on the part of both free farmers and slaveholders, large scale speculation, and easy banking policies.

3. The chart as a whole suggests the expansion of agriculture (and of settlers) into new western lands, the displacement of Native Americans, the impact of feverish speculation on the economy, and the periods of economic expansion in the 1830s and 1850s with the sharp contractions which followed.

Chapter 14 – Cartoon

A Know-Nothing (American Party) cartoon stereotyping the new Irish and German immigrants of the early 1850s as whiskey and beer-drinking ruffians who steal off with the ballot box (presumably to a saloon).

Chapter 15 – Quotation

Abraham Lincoln, Second Inaugural Address, 1865. Delivered less than six weeks before his assassination, the second inaugural is one of the most eloquent and stirring presidential addresses in American history.

Chapter 9 – Map

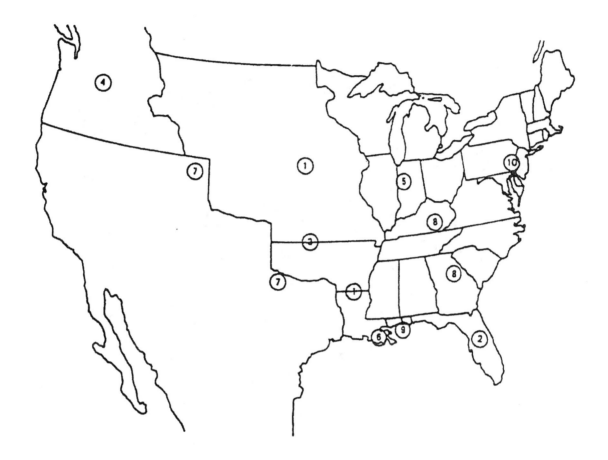

153

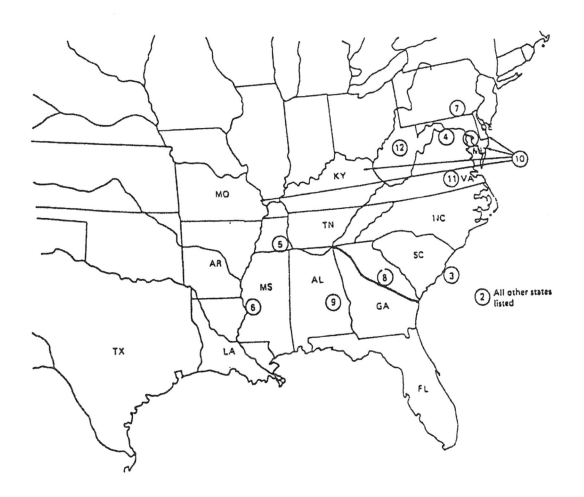